*By A(*

*© Copy*

1

# Learn R Programming

## Fast and Easy

# Table of Contents

4

7

8

# Introduction

## What is R Programming?

R is a free open source software program used for programming statistics and graphics. Statisticians, scientists, analysts, data miners, and mathematicians use R programming to make calculations, conduct polls and surveys. It is highly powerful and extensible language with a programmable environment with command-line scripting. This makes it easier for other users to verify facts and errors, for example evaluating complicated formulas in a spreadsheet. It helps with extracting important statistical data out of data set out of graphics and then making it easier to analyze.

R is considered a data analysis tool, a programming language, a statistics analyzer, an open source software, and collaborative mathematical application for statisticians and computer scientists.

Here is a brief explanation of how R programming is categorized:

- **Data Analysis Tool** – It is a tool used for analyzing statistics, data visualization, and creating data models.

- **Programming Language** – It is used to write scripts and functions. Objects, functions, and operators are used to process, create and calculate data. Only a few lines of code are required to complete a complex calculation.

- **Statistics Analyzer** – Functions are used daily to create graphics, data models, and data. Methods are readily available to perform on-demand statistical research and modeling.

- **Open Source Software** – Users can download and use the language for free, as well as use and modify the source code. This means that anyone can use the methods and algorithms with other applications and systems.

- **Collaborative Mathematical Application** – It allows mathematicians, statistician, computer scientists, and others to collaborate online. Users from various skill-sets and backgrounds can collaborate and communicate with each other on projects.

The R software suite is integrated with features for calculating, data manipulation, and displaying graphics.

R include the following features:

- Effective tools for handling and storing data.
- Effective for developing methods that require interactive data analysis.
- A collection of tools for analyzing data.
- Graphical features for analyzing data and displaying it on the computer or physically.
- S programming features, such as conditionals, user defined functions, and loops.
- Supports matrix arithmetic and procedural programming with functions.
- It contains data structures that include vectors, matrices, arrays, data frames, and lists.
- It includes objects, such as regression models, time series, and geo-spatial coordinates.

**In this Ebook, you will learn more about these features in examples and illustrated.**

# History and Background of R

R programming was created by Ross Ihaka and Robert Gentleman at the University of Auckland in New Zealand. The name R came from the first names of the creators, Ross and Robert. It was developed out of the S programming language, which is still being developed by the *R Development Core Team* in New Zealand.

R is actually a GNU (GNUs Not Unix) project that was written with C, Fortran, and R. It is available for free under the GNU General Public License. It is available to run on Windows, Mac OS X and Unix operating systems.

## What is R used for?

R is used mostly for statistics and data modeling, but it is also used to extract data from graphics for analysis. It contains standard and recommended packages used for storing functions and data sets. R uses features from S, a statistical system that is commonly used by statisticians. S processes statistical analysis in series with only halfway results, but R will provide minimal output and store results for assessment later.

Although R uses the command-line to enter scripts, it also supports several graphical user interfaces (GUIs) to handle graphics and data models. The easiest way to use it though is on a graphics workstation that has a window system. You can create a window environment on a Windows, OS X or a Unix system.

Now that you have some background knowledge of R, it is now time to **Get Started!**

# Getting Started with R: Installing, Starting and Stopping R

## Installing R

To install R on your computer, you will need to download the software at: http://www.r-project.org.

1. On the R-project website click the "**CRAN**" link under the "**Download, Packages**" heading. You will see a list of CRAN mirrors to the right. Select the CRAN Mirror link that is applicable to your region. The "**Comprehensive R Archive Network**" page will open.

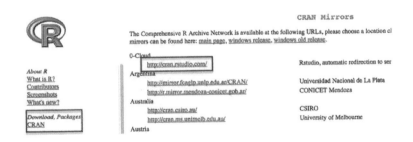

2. On the **"Comprehensive R Archive Network"** page, select one of the following versions and then follow the directions to complete the installation. Select the version that applies to your operating system.

   i.   Download R for Linux

   ii.  Download R for Mac OS X

   iii. Download R for Windows

The Comprehensive R Archive Network

Download and Install R

Precompiled binary distributions of the base system and contributed packages, **Windows and Mac** users most likely want one of these versions of R:

- Download R for Linux
- Download R for (Mac) OS X
- Download R for Windows

R is part of many Linux distributions, you should check with your Linux package management system in addition to the link above.

**Note:** If you are installing R on Windows, select the "base" package. For Mac OS X, select the package that applies to the version of your operating system.

# Starting and Stopping R

To start R, double click on the "**R**" icon on your desktop. The R console will open with some introductory information. Read the information to learn more about R.

Just below the introductory information you will see a prompt or cursor. This is where you will write the commands. You can edit your command use the left and right arrow keys. To stop or close R, type "**q( )**".

```
R version 3.1.1 (2014-07-10) -- "Sock it to Me"
Copyright (C) 2014 The R Foundation for Statistical Computing
Platform: x86_64-apple-darwin13.1.0 (64-bit)

R is free software and comes with ABSOLUTELY NO WARRANTY.
You are welcome to redistribute it under certain conditions.
Type 'license()' or 'licence()' for distribution details.

  Natural language support but running in an English locale

R is a collaborative project with many contributors.
Type 'contributors()' for more information and
'citation()' on how to cite R or R packages in publications.

Type 'demo()' for some demos, 'help()' for on-line help, or
'help.start()' for an HTML browser interface to help.
Type 'q()' to quit R.

[R.app GUI 1.65 (6784) x86_64-apple-darwin13.1.0]

[History restored from /Users/Jeannie/.Rapp.history]
```

```
> 1+1
[1] 2
> |
```

# File Operations and File Formats

R accesses data from .R, .txt, and .csv files. To retrieve the contents of the *"filename.R"* file for example, you would write *"source(filename.R)"* at the command line. When the file is retrieved, the code that is contained in the file will run. R commands are written in plain text and saved in files with the .R extension.

You can run the codes from the command line or in an R instance. You can also access external files that are not in the current folder by writing for example, *"source(R folder/filename.R)"* at the command line. When your create R files, use meaningful names, for example *"weekly_revenue.R"*.

External files are used to store large data objects, which are read as values during an R session. Input files can be modified using tools, such as text editors.

# Writing Code and Text Editors

Writing good R code require practice and some guidance from reference materials, such as <u>Google's R Style Guide</u> and professional coders. It is also easy to write R code in R text editors, such as R Studio, because they help with managing large amounts of data. A statistician, can access programs for data manipulation, reporting statistics, drawing plots and diagrams with just few clicks.

## Writing R Code

The first thing that you should remember when writing code, is to use proper punctuation. There are various ways to punctuate your code, but you should be consistent. This helps other readers to understand your style. You may need to adjust your style to meet basic standards of code writing.

Here are some tips for writing good code in R:

- **File names** – Filenames should end with the R extension, for example *"filename.r"* and try not to capitalize unnecessarily because some operating systems are case sensitive. Files that need to run in sequence, use a number prefix before them, for example:

```
1_daily_revenue.R

2_weekly_revenue.R

3_monthly_revenue.R
```

- **Variable and Function names** – Write variable and function names in lowercase letters and use an underscore to separate words, for example "*room_rate*". Variable names should be nouns and function names should be verbs. Try not to use names of existing or predefined functions and variables. You don't want to confuse your readers.

- **Spaces** – Spaces are placed between infix operators (+, =, -), after a comma, before left parentheses (except in function calls), and always put a space after a comma. It is ok to put extra spaces between assignments (<-) and equal signs (=) to make your code clear and readable. Do not use spaces around code in parentheses, square brackets, :, ::, and :::.
Here are some examples of when to use spaces and when not to use spaces:

```
sum(1, 3, 5) - No spacing in
function calls, except after commas.
23 + 5 - 4  - Spaces between infix
operators.
sum::get  - No spaces with
colons (:) double colons (::) or
triple colons (:::).
total = a + b + c - Extra
spacing to improve readability and
alignment.
```

```
coordinates[5,1]  -  No spaces
around codes in brackets.
```

- **Curly braces** – Opening and closing curly braces should have their own lines and must be followed by a new line. If a closing curly brace is followed by an else, it does not need its own line. Codes in curly braces must be indented.

Here is an example of how to write code with curly braces.

```
if (x < 5 && sum)

    {   write("X is a Coordinate")

}

if (y == 0)

    {   get(y) } else { x > y }
```

- **Line statements** – You can write short statements in the same line, but try to limit code to about 80 characters per line.

```
if (x < 5 && sum) write("X is a
Coordinate")
```

- **Indenting Code** – Use two spaces when you are indenting code and do not use tabs or mix tabs and

21

spaces. However, if a function definition uses multiple lines, then indent the second line, for example:

```
calculate(x = "a + b",
              y = "40 - 19",
              z = "30 + 2 - 9")
```

- **Functions** – Use verbs for function names, use the return() function for early returns, and use about 20 – 30 lines maximum on a single screen.

- **Comments** – Always comment each line of your code with the comment symbol (#). Use multiple dashes (--) or (=) to divide your file, so it can be readable. You can place comments anywhere in the file.

```
# Calculate weekly numbers ---------
-
# Plot coordinates ----------------
```

Writing code correctly comes with practice, but you can follow these simple guidelines to get you started.

## R Text Editors

It is much easier to write code in a GUI (Graphical User Interface) because it is much faster and simpler, although some statisticians and computer scientists prefer to write it in the command line of the R console. For those who prefer to write R in a separate file, this is when a text editor is required. A text editor in the operating system is often used, but specialized editors provide integrations for R programming.

The following is a list of text editors for R programming:

- **Tinn-R** – This is and easy to use GUI text editor for R programming in Windows.

- **RKward** – An easy to R text editor that works with GNU/Linux, Windows, and Mac OS X environments. It is an extensible IDE/GUI for R.

- **RStudio** – This is a user-friendly tool that is similar to RKward, but easier to work with. It also works on Mac OS X, Windows, and Linux environments.

- **JGR** – This is like RStudio with similar GUI that integrates with the R command line console.

- **Emacs with ESS ("Emacs Speaks Statistics)** – This is add on package that works with Unix, Linux, Windows and Mac OS X environments.

There are several text editors that you can use to write R, but these are widely used by statisticians and computer scientists.

# Basic R Syntax

R is a simple syntax that is an expression language. It is a UNIX package that is case sensitive, therefore "A" is not the same as "a" when referring to variables. The syntax symbols may vary based on the country and the operating system. All alphanumeric symbols are allowed (this includes accent letters used in some countries).

Simple commands are either expressions or assignments.

```
    1  +  1  -   This  is  an
expression.

      mean_average <- average(1, 5,
7, 19) - This is an assignment
```

Commands are separated with a semi-colon or a new line. Simple commands are typically grouped with open and close curly braces ({ }). When a command is incomplete, R will insert a prompt by default.

The following are different types of expressions used in R:

- **Constants** – Constants are any number or text type in the R console. There are five types of constants; integers, logical, string, numeric, and complex. Here is an example of a string constant:

```
"R programming!"
```

- **Arithmetic operators** - Arithmetic operators, such as addition (+), subtraction (-), division (/), multiplication (*), integer division (%/%), remainder for integer division (%% - modulo arithmetic) and exponentiation (^) are standard operators used in R programming.

  Here is an example of an addition operation:

  ```
  1 + 1
  ```

- **Logical and Comparison operators** – Logical operators, such as || (or) and && (and) are used to combine to logical values to get a logical result. The ! (not) is the negation of a logical value. Comparison operators (<, >, <=, >=, ==, and !=) are used to compare values in vectors to determine if one vector is larger, smaller or equal to another. The %in% operator is use to determine a match between a left and right operand. This produces a logical vector.

  Here is an example of a greater than operation:

  ```
  a > 6
  ```

- **Function calls** – Function calls have any number of arguments with the same name, for example functionName(argument1,              argument2). Here is an example of a function call:

```
sqrt(7*3+3)
```

- **Symbols and assignments** – If it is not a digit or a special keyword, then it is a symbol. Values can be assigned       with       the       <-       operator. Here is an example of an assignment:

```
combineA <- c(3,5,7,9)
```

- **Loops** - A loop is used to repeat a group of expressions. For loops are used to run expressions for a specific number of times. The expressions run in sequence. While loops run until the condition becomes FALSE and should produce a single logical                                          value. Here is an example of a for loop:

```
for (x in 1:20)

{ sqr[x]^2 }
```

- **Conditional expressions** – Conditional expressions are used to make expressions dependent on a condition. The condition should produce a single logical value and should only run if the condition is TRUE. Curly braces may or may not be use. R uses if, else statements to write conditional expressions. Here is an example of a conditional expression:

```
if( x < 0.07)

{ x <- x * 2

sqrt(x) }
```

# Files

Files in R typically have extensions on the filenames, for example **'datafile.csv'**. The '.csv' is the extension. Although R does not recognize extensions it is helpful for users to know the difference. Some primary file extensions used in R programming include '. rda', '.r', '.txt', and '.csv'.

Here is a brief explanation of the different file types:

- **.RDA files** – These are saved R objects that are used to attaching and loading files. They use the .rda or .RData extension. Files with the. RData and the .rda extension are the same.

- **.R files** – These files are created inside the R editor by the dump function. They include R commands. Some R files may also have the .q extension.

- **.TXT files** – These are text files that are used to store datasets. R uses the `read.table()` function and the `write.table()` function. R uses the `read.table()` for data input and reading from text files. It then automatically creates a data frame with it. The `write.table()` function on the other hand is used to create the text files.

- **.CSV files** – CSV or Comma Separated Values files are common data file types inputted with the `read.csv()` function.

R files typically store large amounts of data or data objects instead of being inputted from the keyboard. You can enter small data objects in the R console at the command prompt, but it is best to store large data objects in .rda, .r, .txt, .csv, and other data files. You can then use the read and write functions to read and write data into R.

## Reading Files with Functions

R reads large data objects as values from external files. Although, you can enter small amounts of data at the keyboard in an R programming session, the environment is very simplistic and would take a long time to enter large amounts of data. Therefore, it is better that you modify input files using file editors to accommodate the requirements of the language.

Variables and other types of data should be stored in data frames and then read with the `read.table()` function or with the older input function called `scan()`. The `read.table()` function is more commonly used to read in rectangular data, but it is recommended that you use the `scan()` function to read very large numerical matrices.

In the following section, you will learn more about the `read.table()` function and how to use it with different arguments to read various types of data files. We will also look at how to use the `scan()` and `read.csv()` functions.

If you would like to

## Read.table() function

The `read.table()` function is used to read data from an external file into R. It supports several arguments, but it only needs the filename to read data into R. You can read the entire data from an external file or you can specify how you would like to read the data using arguments.

To read the data from the external file, you will need to ensure that the data is displayed in a specific way. The first line of the data must have the name of each variable in a row. Below each variable name, you should have the values for each of the variables. If the values are omitted, R assumes that this was intentional. The numeric values in

31

the data file are read as numeric and non-numeric variables. You can always change it if necessary.

Here is an example of an external data file, let us call it *"Inventory.data"*. This file includes a column with row labels (example 01).

You do not have to include a row label column. Instead, you can allow R to use the default row labels. Data with variable names and row labels may look like the following example:

```
Price        Item        Code
        Status <- This is the variable
name

01    20.00      Book        010A
      Sold

02    1.00       Pen         9290
      Order

03    .50        Eraser      30Q1
      Pending
```

To read the entire contents of the data file *"Inventory.data"*, you would use the read.table() function to read the data frame directly into R, using the following statement.

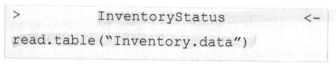

```
>              InventoryStatus        <-
read.table("Inventory.data")
```

If you choose to omit the row label column from the data file, you would need to include the header argument when reading the data. This is how you would read the data with the header and a separator.

```
> InventoryStatus <-
read.table("Inventory.data",
header=TRUE, sep="")
```

Both statements assign the contents of a file to an object. The data in the "Inventory.data" file is assigned to the "InventoryStatus" object.

Here is an explanation of the statements:

- **InventoryStatus** – This is the object that will store the contents of the "Inventory.data".

- **read.table()** – The read.table() function requires an external file. In this case it contains the "Inventory.data" file.

- **header=TRUE** – This is used if the file does not contain any row labels, but has the names of the variables in the first line. The variables specify that the file contain headings. When a file does not contain a column for the row labels, then default row labels are assigned.

- **sep=""** – This is the field separator used for separating the files in the file. The pair of quotations represents whitespaces and can have one or more spaces, lines, tabs, or carriage returns. You can use it in the following ways:
  - **Space delimited data** – Use **sep=" "** for space delimited data.
  - **Tab delimited data** – Use **sep="\t"** for tab delimited data.
  - **New line delimited data** – Use **"sep="\n"** for new line delimited data.

> **Note:** Delimited data or text is a simple file format that is separated by certain characters. The text is usually individual and the characters used are called delimiters.

## Variations of read.table()

The `read.table()` function is used in various ways to read data into R from a rectangular grid. Various arguments are used inside the function to manipulate different types of data.

The following is a list of variations of the `read.table()` function:

1. **Encoding** – When a file contains non-ASCII characters, you should ensure that it is read correctly. If you are reading Latin-1 files in the UTF-8 location, you would need to use the following statement. It will work for Latin-1 strings, but it may not work for Chinese/Russian/Greek and similar regions. The fileEncoding argument is used to designate these types of files.

   ```
   read.table("Inventory.data",
   fileEncoding="latin1")
   ```

2. **Header** – The header argument should be used when the file only contains variable names. When R recognizes that there are no row labels, then it will set header = TRUE. If you have a file without row labels, you can read the data with something similar to the following statement.

   ```
   read.table("Inventory.data",
   header=TRUE, row.names=1)
   ```

3. **Separator** – The default separators, sep =""" and sep ="\t", is used to create white spaces in files. This is used to create spaces, tabs, or newlines. The type of separator used will determine the input based on the quote argument. The following statement uses the new line separator. This means the when the data is read into R, each value will be placed on a new line.

```
InventoryStatus                    <-
read.table("Inventory.data",
header=TRUE, sep="/n")
```

4. **Missing Values** – It is assumed by default that the file contains missing values and uses NA to represent those missing values. If there are missing numeric values in the columns, the NaN, Inf, and the –Inf character strings are displayed.

Empty fields or missing values maybe displayed like the following:

| | Price | Item | Code |
|---|---|---|---|
| | | Status | |
| 01 | 20.00 | Book | 010A |
| | Sold | | |
| 02 | 1.00 | Pen | **NaN** |
| | **NA** | | |

36

```
03    .50        Eraser       30Q1
      Pending
```

5. **Unfilled lines** – When a file is exported from a spreadsheet, there might be some empty fields with missing separators. To read these files, use set fill = TRUE.

```
InventoryStatus                      <-
read.table("Inventory.data",
header=TRUE, fill=TRUE)
```

6. **White spaces** – If there is a separator, leading, or a trailing whites spaces in a character field, you can strip the space with the strip.white = TRUE argument.

```
InventoryStatus                      <-
read.table("Inventory.data",
header=TRUE, strip.white=TRUE)
```

7. **Blank lines** – The read.table() function ignores empty lines by default, but you can change it by declaring blank.lines.skip=FALSE. This only works with fill=TRUE.

```
InventoryStatus                         <-
read.table("Inventory.data",
header=TRUE,                    fill=TRUE,
blank.lines.skip=FALSE)
```

8. **Classes** – The `read.table()` by default reads the columns as character vectors and then choose a class for each variable in the file. It checks for integers, logical numbers, numeric values, and complex variables. If there are missing entries, then the variables are converted to a factor. The colClasses used in the following statement to convert the character vectors to factors in the "*Inventory.data*" file.

```
read.table("Inventory.data",   header
= TRUE, colClasses = classes)
```

9. **Comments** – The `read.table()` function by default uses the '#' to create comments. When R sees the '#' in a quoted string, it ignores the rest of the line. If there are white spaces with a comment, the comment is treated as a blank line. When there are no comments in the file, the comment.char=""""

syntax is used like how it is used in the following statement.

```
read.table("Inventory.data",
comment.char="#")
```

10. **Escape and Backslash** – Operating systems have different ways of using the backslash and escape keys in text files. However, Windows uses the backslash in path names. In R, the backslash is optional in data files. When `read.table()` uses allowEscapes, which is false by default, the backslashes are then interpreted as escapes quotes. Escape arguments are interpreted with control characters, such as \a, \b, \f, \n, and \r.

11. **Convenience functions** – The `read.csv()` and `read.delim()` functions provide arguments to the `read.table()` function for tab delimited and CSV files that are exported from spreadsheets in English speaking locations.

# Read.csv() function

The read.csv() function is used to read a data file with the "comma separated values" (csv) format. CSV files contain values with numbers and letters separated with a comma. The first row of the file usually contains label names for differentiating the columns for the values.

Here is an example of a CSV with some data. It contains three columns and three rows of data. The data file is called **"products.csv"**. The columns are labeled **"Product"**, **"Price"**, and **"Quantity"**. It is assumed that the rows have three products, **"Book"**, **"Stationary"**, and, **"Toy"**.

Here is how the data file might look with the data.

| Product | Price | Quantity |
| --- | --- | --- |
| Book | 9.99 | 2 |
| Stationary | 3.00 | 6 |
| Toy | 24.00 | 3 |

To read the data file, you will need to use the "**read.csv**" command. The command must have at least one argument, but you can have three or more arguments. In the following example, the first argument is the name of the data file, the second argument the first row for the labels, and the third argument specifies that there is a comma between each line.

Here is how you can read the data and assign it to the "**inventoryinfo**" variable with three arguments.

```
> inventoryinfo <-
read.csv(file="products.csv",head=TR
UE,sep=",")
```

The variable "**inventoryinfo**" contains three columns with data. A name is assigned to each column. The column names are on the first line within the file. To access each column, use the "**$**" to differentiate the names of the columns. For example, if you would like to access the data in the **"Price"** column, you would use the following command:

```
> inventoryinfo$Price
```

If you are not sure which column in the data file you would like to access use "**names**" command to list all the names of the columns in the data file. Here is an example of how you would use the "**names**" command:

```
> names(inventoryinfo)
```

The "**summary**" command can also be used to call the data from a CSV data file. It is used after the data file is assigned to a variable. Here is how you would use the '**summary**' command.

```
> summary(inventoryinfo)
```

If the file is located in a specific directory or folder, you will need to specify the directory and the folder name to retrieve the file. The naming conventions for retrieving files from folders and directories are located in the help folder. To view the list of options for retrieving files, use the help(read.csv) command.

> **Note:** If you are using a Windows operating system, you will need to use two backslashes ("\\") to access the file.

If you are unable to find the file, you maybe looking in the wrong folder or directory. Use the *dir()* command to locate the file, as well as identify a file, if you forgot the filename. The *getwd()* command will display the directory that you are currently working with.

If you have data in an excel spreadsheet, you can convert it to a CSV file, by removing the top row of the spreadsheet file and then save it as a ".csv" file. Excel allows you to save its spreadsheets as CSV files. To better understand how R stores data, open the CSV file in Excel.

After you convert the spreadsheet into a CSV file, you can read it into a variable as normal. For example, if you converted an Excel file called "**datainventory.xls**" into "**datainventory.csv**", you can read it into the variable "**data**" by using the following command:

```
> data <-
read.csv(file="datainventory.csv",he
ader=TRUE,sep=",");
```

This example creates a new variable called "**data**". When you enter "**data**" at the prompt, all the data stored in the variable will be displayed.

Here is how you would use the **"attributes"** command to determine the **"data"** variable type, for example. This will list the different ways R describes the variable.

```
> attributes (data)
```

## Scan() function

The scan() function is used to read various types of data or data objects, for example data vectors. You can customize the command to read specific data. The command waits for input from the user and then returns the value entered at the prompt. To read three data vectors from a data file called **"datavectors.dat"**, you would use the following command with the **"datav"** variable, for example.

```
> datav <- scan("datavectors.dat",
list("",1,1))
```

The second argument, *list("",0,0)* is a dummy or false structure for creating the three vectors that will be read into the "**datav**" variable. The data items are separated into the three vectors, using the following command:

```
> datalabel <- datav[[1]]; x <-
datav[[2]]; y <- datav[[3]]
```

Notice that the three vectors are stored in the "**datalabel**" variable, which will be used to read in the vectors. This is how you would access the vectors with the scan() function.

```
> datav <- scan("datavectors.dat",
list(id="", x=1, y=1))
```

To access the variables separately, use the "**$**" symbol.

```
> datalabel <- datav$id; x <-
datav$x; y <- datav$y
```

# Importing & Reading Files

There are various file formats that can be imported into R. Earlier we discussed reading CSV and XLS files into R. Here we will revisit these files, as well as other file formats. We will discuss importing file formats such as Minitab, SPSS, and TXT files.

## Excel Files

Most of the time the data that you would like to import is in Excel format. Since most organizations use Excel files, you will need to understand how to use various methods for importing Excel data in R. These methods will import Excel data into R before you start using it. They have their advantages and disadvantages, but they all read data from an Excel spreadsheet and return the data in a data frame into R.

Here is an overview of the some of the methods used to read data from an Excel spreadsheet into R.

1. **Save Excel files as Text** – You can save Excel files into CSV format in an Excel spreadsheet or with an external tool that allow batch processing. You can then use the **"read.table()"** function to import the text format (that is CSV).

```
> txt <- read.table("textfile.csv",
header = TRUE)
```

2. **Copy and Paste Data from Excel** – This is one of the easiest solution or method, but you will need to open the Excel file, select the data, and then copy with the copy and paste commands or with the copy and paste options available in Excel. You can use this method when you would like to get things done quickly. This requires the **"read.table()"** function.

```
> txt <- read.table("clipboard")
```

3. **Excel ODBC driver** – This method requires the installation of the Excel Open Database Connectivity (ODBC) driver. This method is not well recommended because it requires several lines of code to install the drive, connect with the Excel file, and read the file. This method is used with Microsoft Windows and 32-bit R.

The following example shows how to establish a connection, get the data sheet, and close the connection to the Excel file.

First, open a connection to the Excel file.

```
> require(RODBC)
> connFile <- odbcConnectExcel("excelFile.xlsx")
#open a connection
```

Second, display and read the data sheet.

```
> sqlTables(connFile) $tableName, "Sheet1")

> txt <- sqlFetch(connFile,"Sheet1")
# display all data sheets
> txt <- sqlQuery(connFile, "select * from [Sheet1 $]") # read data sheet
```

Third, close the connection to the file.

```
> close(connFile) # close the connection
```

4. **Gdata package** - The gdata package is a cross platform solution that works on Windows, Mac OS, and Linux operating systems. The gdata package requires that you install Perl libraries, which should already be available on Linux and Max systems. However, it may require additional steps for Windows platforms.

```
> require(gdata)
```

```
> txt <- read.xls("excelFile.xlsx",
datasheet = 1, header = TRUE)
```

5. **xlsReadWrite package**

The xlsReadWrite package does not support xlsx files and it is not widely use these days, but it is a method that can used. It requires the use of third party code from GitHub and CRAN and only works on Windows platforms.

```
> require(xlsReadWrite)

> xls.getshlib()

> txt <- read.xls("excelFile.xlsx",
datasheet = 1)
```

**XLConnect package-** The XLConnect package that is a Java based solution that works across most platforms. This works best with small data sets. If you are working with large data sets, it may take a long time.

```
>                    require(XLConnect)
>           xlsFile              <-
loadWorkbook("excelFile.xlsx")

>   txt   <-   readWroksheet(xlsFile,
datasheet = "Sheet1", header = TRUE)
```

It is preferable to import Excel files as CSV files using the "**read.table()**" function mentioned in (1) and in the "**Reading Files with Functions**" section. It is the easiest way to import xlsx files into R. However, if you have small data sets, you can use the XLConnect method.

## Minitab Files

Minitab files contain data stored as the Minitab Portable Worksheet format. It uses the "**read.mtp**" file to read the xlsx file. The file returns a list with one component for each column, matrix, or constant that is stored in the Minitab worksheet. The process requires that you first load the "**foreign**" package, call the "**read.mtp**" function, and then read in the ".**mtp**" file.

First, load the "**foreign**" package.

```
> library(foreign)
```

Second, call the "**read.mtp**" file.

```
> help(read.mtp)
```

Third, read the ".**mtp**" file.

```
> myfile <- read.mtp ("myfile.mtp")
```

## SPSS File

An SPSS file or Statistical Package for the Social Sciences is a file format used to store data for statistical analysis. The file is stored with the ".sav" extension. SPSS files are data files that are opened with the "read.spps" function from the "foreign" package. The "to.data.frame" argument is used inside the function to determine if a data frame will be returned.

The following process shows how to load, access, and read spss files.

First, load the "foreign" package.

```
> library(foreign)
```

Second, access the "read.spss function.

```
> help(read.spss)
```

Third, read the ".sav" file.

```
myfile <- read.spss("dataFile.sav",
to.data.frame=TRUE)
```

## Built-in datasets

There are over 100 built-in datasets listed in the "datasets" package. To see the list of datasets, enter data()" at the command prompt. This will list the data sets by their names in alphabetic order. It will also load the data sets into memory for statistical analysis. For example, if you would like to load the **"infert"** data set into memory, you would enter the following at the command prompt.

```
> data(infert)
```

# Symbols and Assignments

## R Symbols

When you create a new variable, it must have a name that typically references a value. The name is actually a symbol, which evaluates the value that is returned. A symbol is also an R object and can be manipulated the same way as objects. Symbols refer to an R object and the name of an R object is a symbol.

The following example shows the symbol "**x**" and the value "**6**" that is assigned or associated with the symbol or variable.

```
x <- 6

x

[1] 6
```

You can also use a symbol to create functions. In other words, functions can be assigned to a symbol, but it is not necessary. Symbols in a function can be bound or unbound. There three types of symbols within a function. They are formal parameters or formal arguments, local variable, and free variables. Formal arguments within a function are called bound symbols. They are within the body of the function. All other symbols in the body are either local or unbound variables.

Since R is an expression language that is case sensitive, you need to be careful when using different symbols, such as variable names. You should also consider the type of operating system and country that you reside when using a set of R symbols. Typically, alphanumeric symbols such as periods (.), and underscores (_) are allowed. However, there are restrictions. A name must start with a period (.) or a letter. If a name starts with a period (.), then the second character must not be a number. You can have name that is unlimited in length.

Objects can be referred with symbols, which are actually objects. A symbol is considered an object in R. Symbols can be used in the same way as other objects and are also considered variable names. In an environment, there is a set of symbol-value pairs and R looks for symbols within the frame of the environment. The symbols within the environment contain a search list that is searched sequentially for a matching symbol. If the symbol is located, then the value is returned. Therefore, if you assign the same environment to many symbols and change one of them, the other symbols will be changed as well.

When you create a variable name, you actually create a symbol. The name is the symbol. They usually contain a value, which is evaluated and returned. In the following example "x" has the value "3", where "x" is the symbol and "3" is the value. The value here is assigned to the symbol.

```
> x <- 3
```

Values returned with "for", "while", and "repeat" loops can assign their results to symbols. Also, argument lists or formal arguments in functions can be considered symbols. In this case, symbols are expressions.

## R Assignments

R assignments evaluate expressions and passes values to variables. However, the result is not automatically displayed. You have to call the variable name to see the results.

In R, most actions performed in R are caused by function calls. Function calls return a value and often requires a name to be assigned to that value. There are two ways that you can assign a value. You can assign a value using assignment operators. The less than and minus sign together (<-) and the equal sign (=) are the assignment operators used to assign values to variable names.

The = operator is an alternative to using the less than and minus (<-) assignment operators. The <- operator can be used any place in R, but the = operator can only be used in an expression entered at the command line or in a sub expression with brackets. Both operators, point to the object receiving the value in the expression and are assigned into the environment where they are evaluated.

Here is an example of how you would create an assignment with the less than and minus (<-) assignment operators.

```
> squarey <- sqrt(x*x+2)
```

Here is how you would create an assignment with the equal sign (=).

```
> squarey = sqrt(x*x+2)
```

In both cases, the value of the "**sqrt(x*x+2)**" expression is stored in the variable name "**squarey**". When the variable "**squarey**" is executed, it will become an object within the environment. It does not matter which assignment symbol you use, it is up to you and based on your preference. You can use either one. Just remember that R is case-sensitive.

So if you use **"squareY"**, it will be different from **"squarey"**. These two names are different in the eyes of R. You should also be aware that R does not display any information when you make an assignment. You will need to enter the name of the variable at the command line and press enter. For example, if you want to display the results you will need to do the following:

```
squarey <- sqrt (1*2+2)

squarey

[1] 2
```

After you assign the variable, you call the variable name to display the value that is assigned to the variable.

Assignment statements may only include a single expression without a function.

Here is an example of an assignment with a single expression.

```
y <- 10 + 2
```

Assignments are also made in another way, by changing the direction of the less than and minus operators (<-) to (->). An assignment with the operators in the other direction may look like the following statement:

```
> 10 + 2 -> y
```

An assignment evaluates expressions and passes the values to variables, but it is not necessarily automatically displayed or printed. Assignment statements with functions can have any number of arguments. The following example shows an assignment statement with several arguments. It shows the w() function with 4 numbers.

```
> x <- w(23, 3, 4, 1)
```

The assignment operator (<-) in this case can be substituted for the equal (=) operator. Assignments can also be used with the assign() function. This is the same as the assignment statement with the w() function.

The following example shows you how to use the assign() function. This is an alternative method or equivalent method to the w() function.

```
> assign("x", f(23, 3, 4, 1))
```

The left assignment operator (<-) is considered the short to using the assign() function. As previously learned, assignment operators can be used in the opposite direction. For example, instead of using the left assignment operator (<-), you can use the right assignment operator.

The following example shows you how to use the right assignment (->) operator for the w() function.

```
> w(23, 3, 4, 1) -> x
```

## Assignments with Functions

The assignment operators <<- and ->> are used to create assignments with functions only. They are also used to search for the same definition with the same variable name within a parent environment. If the variable is found and it is not locked, then the value is redefined. If the variable is not found, the assignment will be used in the global environment.

To use the <<- operators, you would type the following, for example:

```
y <<- mean(10 + 2)
```

To use the ->> operators, you would type the following, for example:

```
mean(10 + 2) ->> y
```

> **Note:** Any assignments performed within the function are local and temporary. This means that they are lost after the user exits the function. Therefore, the assignment Y <- sqrt(Y) will not affect the value of the argument when it is called.

## Super, Subset and Complex Assignments

Super assignment operators are used to create global and permanent assignments within functions. The super assignment operator (<<-) or the assign9) function is used under these circumstances.

When it comes to subset assignments, it can be complex in specific cases. The following statement is an example of a complex assignment:

```
x[1:4] <- 22:12
```

The result from this statement is similar to the following:

```
'*prm*' <- x

x      <-      "[<-"('*prm*',      1:4,
value=22:12)

val('*prm*')
```

In the above statement, you will see that the index is converted to a numeric index and then replaced with a sequential numeric index. The existing variable "*prm*" will be overwritten and deleted, but the variable name must not be used in the code.

You do not have to use the open bracket ([) with the left

assignment operator. Instead, you can use a replacement function with the left assignment operator. The last argument with the val() function is the value that will be assigned.

The following example shows how you can use a replacement function:

```
numbers(x) <- c("a","b")
```

The result from the function statement is similar to the following:

```
'*prm*' <- x

x           <-          "numbers<-"('*prm*',
value=c("a","b"))

val('*prm*')
```

Complex assignments can be evaluated recursively with nesting.

Here is a complex assignment that uses nesting:

```
numbers(x)[4] <- "Four"
```

This statement is similar to the following:

```
'*prm*' <- x
```

```
x          <-          "numbers<-"('*prm*',
value="[<-"(numbers('*prm*'),        4,
value="Four"))

  val('*prm*')
```

You can also use the double left super assignment (<<-)
instead of the single left single assignment (<-) to create a
complex assignment.

```
numbers(x)[4] <<- "Four"
```

This statement is equivalent to the following:

```
'*prm*'              <<-              get(x,
envir=parent.env(), inherits=TRUE)

    numbers('*prm*')[4] <- "Four"

    x <<- '*prm*'

    val('*prm*')
```

# Control Structures

Control structures are used to control the flow of statements to be executed by the R interpreter. They include conditional statements and loops. R computes these statements by sequentially evaluating each one. Statements can be either separated by a semi-colon or a new line. Semi-colons are used to create separate statements. They help the interpreter to differentiate the statements and make the statements more understandable and readable to the programmer. Both semi-colons and new lines designate the end of a statement. If the statements are incomplete, the interpreter ignores it and if the programming session is interactive, the prompt changes from the right arrow (>) to the plus sign (+).

The following example shows how a session reacts when it is interactive.

```
> x <- 0; x + 7
[1] 7
```

When the interpreter detects a complete statement, it evaluates it and returns a value. The result that is returned is considered the value of the statement. This value can be assigned to a symbol.

Statements within control structures are grouped with open braces ({) and closed braces (}). Statements enclosed in braces are called blocks. Blocks are read after a closing brace and a single statement is read when a new line is created at the end of a complete statement. In a nutshell, statements are referred to a single statements or a block.

Here is an example of a statement that is enclosed in braces.

```
>       {       x       <-      0
>       +       x       +       4       }
[1]  4
```

R uses if, if/else, while, repeat, and for control structures to produce results for conditional and repetitive statements.

The following syntaxes will show you how to write the applicable control structures:

- if -- if (condition) expression; for example:

```
if(x>y)
{ print (X is greater than Y) }
```

- if/else – if (condition) expression1 else expression2;

for example:

```
if                                  (2==1)
{print(Yes)}
  else print(No)
```

- while – while(condition) expression; for example:

```
x                    <-              1
while(x              <              4)
{ x <- x + 2 print(x) }
```

- repeat – repeat expression; for example:

```
x                    <-              1
repeat    {    x    <-    x    +    1
print(z) break() }
```

- for – for (variables in sequence) statement; for example

```
for    (value    in    seq(0,1,by=0.3))
  {        result(value,"\n");    }
```

These expressions in the above control structure are normally referred to as compound expressions. In the while, repeat and for loop constructs you can use a break to terminate the loop and next to go to the next iteration (repetition of the process).

The constructs for "**if**", "**while**", "**repeat**", "**for**", "**break**", and "**next**" control structures are stored internally as functions.

## Conditional and Repetitive Executions

R uses conditional and repetitive constructions to evaluate single and multiple values. It uses **"if"** and **"if/else"** statements to evaluate single logical values to produce valid results.

## Conditional Execution

Conditional executions are conditional constructions that uses the following syntax:

```
if      (expression1)      expression2
else expression3
```

The **"if/else"** syntax shows that **"expression1"** must be evaluated to a single value.

The operators AND(&&) and OR(||) are often used in "if" statements. The single AND(&) and OR(|) operators on the other hand applies to vectors based on elements. The AND (&&) and OR (||) operators, however apply to vectors of a single length, and only evaluates the second expression if necessary.

R uses a vector based if/else construct called an ifelse

function. It uses the following syntax:

```
ifelse(condition, x, y)
```

The **"ifelse"** function returns a vector with the length of the longest argument. It contains elements a[i] and b[i], where [i] is true, else execute b[i].

## Repetitive Execution

Repetitive executions involve for loops, repeat and while constructions.

The "for" loop uses the following syntax:

```
for (variable_name in expression1)
expression2
```

The "for" loop syntax has the loop variable as **"variable_name"** and the vector expression as " **expression1"**. The vector expression often has a sequence that looks 1:20(1 row; 20 vectors). The grouped expression is **"expression2"**, which is evaluated repeatedly through the values of the vector result of **"expression1"**.

If you have an example and you have **"vec"** as a vector of class indicators. If you wish to produce separate x and y plots in the classes, you could use the coplot() function.

This will produce an array of plots that corresponds to each level of the factor. You could also do this, by using all the plots on one display.

The following example shows how to use all the plots on one display:

```
> xc <- split(x, vec)
> yc <- split(y, vec)
for (i in 1:length(yc))
{ plot(xc[[i]], yc[[i]])
abline(lsfit(xc[[i]],
yc[[i]])) }
```

The split() function produces a list of vectors that is obtained by splitting the larger vector based on the classes specified by the vector. This function is often used in boxplots.

**Important:** In R code, "for" loops are not used regularly in compiled languages. Codes that look at the entire object are apparently better and faster.

Other types of loops used in R includes repeat and while statements. The break statement is used with loops to terminate/end an action. It is the only way that you can terminate repeat loops. The next statement is used to end a specific cycle and move to the "**next**".

> **Note:** Control statements are typically used with functions.

## Iteration

In this section you will briefly learn about iteration. This is an important topic for programmers because it is used to control the flow of elements within a program, as well as analyzing data. In data analysis iterative statements powers procedures for calculating complex datasets and advanced mathematical calculations relating to statistics.

### Loops and Vectorization

R allows you to create loops and calculate vectors using iteration in R. Loops are used to repeat an operation for a specific number of times. In the following example, you will see how a simple for loop is created.

```
>        for       (i      in       1:n)
>    {  cat("Name   #",   i,   "\n")   }
[1]  Name  #  1    Name  #  2    Name  #  3
Name  #  4
```

In the above example of the for loop, the counter is set and the loop runs for "n" number of times. The result shows that the loop iterated 4 times. The loop actually created one line of output for each value of n=(1, 2, 3) that is passed through the index "I". The final element in the in the string concatenation is "\n" – a new line break is implemented.

This example shows how iteration works with a for loop. You will learn more about "**for**" loops later on in this chapter.

The example can be replaced by applying the function with the three elements of the vector I, , 2, 3. 4. You can do this because the paste() function is vectored. This method can be used to substitute looping in many situations. In the above example, you would replace "**cat("Name #", i, "\n")**" with "**paste(Country #", 1:4)**". This is vectored approach.

The while loop is similar to the "for" loop and uses iteration until a condition is either true or false. You may also say that the while loop condition is true until it is not.

Pay close attention when writing the conditions, because the loop can iterate indefinitely. An indefinite loop is only necessary under special circumstances.

Here is an example of a while loop:

```
i                    <-           5
while (i > 0) { print(i <- i - 1) }
[1]  4  [1]  3  [1]  2  [1]  1  [1]  0 //
output
```

In the above example of the while loop, the counter is set (i<-5) and is decreased by 1 until it gets to 0.

There are more complex ways to solve problems with while loops, like searching for the solution to a **"finding-the-number"** fame. This is called the "brute force" approach (no shortcuts). You will learn more about writing while loops later on in this chapter.

There are other loops that are sequentially exhaustive and can become very intensive to calculate when they iterate through arrays with values. When this happens, you may need to optimize the code and use several processors to reduce the response time of the loop.

You can iteratively execute a loop or vectorize the loop. Most loops can be replaced with vectorization because it is more efficient to manage the data this way. Vectorized functions are used in R because they run faster than memory-intensive loops with built-in code. The idea is to apply a specific function instead of instructing R to apply the function separately.

The following examples will show you how to write an iterative loop and a vectorized loop.

```
// An iterative loop
square i,
square i + 1,
square i + 2,
for (i in 1:2) print(i^2)
[1] 1 [1] 4
```

```
// A vectorized loop
define i = { 1, 2 }
(1:2)^2
[1] 1 4
```

In the above example, the vector is 1, 2. The square function is used to evaluate the vectors, which returns the results for the vector. Be aware that many of the functions in R accept vectors as arguments, which makes it easier to calculate. This helps to resolve potential conflicts. In the following examples, you will see how combination vectors are used.

```
// This example shows two possible
conflicts in a single combination.
prod(1:2)/prod(1:2)
[1] 1
```

```
// This example shows 3 possible
combinations.
prod(1:3)/(prod(1:2)   *   prod(1:1))
[1] 3
```

```
//This example shows 6 possible
combinations.
prod(1:4)/(prod  (1:2)  *  prod(1:2))
[1] 6
```

The structure of this function is called the "**explosive roommate function**". It looks at the number of potential conflicts that is possible with each "roommate" that is affecting the other. The code calculates the value using the following equation: $\frac{n!}{k!(n-k)!}$, where $n$ is the number of roommates and $k = 2$. The function can be used to calculate increasing numbers. You can also plot part of the function by creating a vector of values and apply the combinations. It is done by using the sapply() function. This is the vectorized equivalent of the **"for"** loop.

The following example shows the **"explosive roommate function"** written by Francis Smart.

```
// Explosive roommates function.
explosive_roommates   =   function(n)
prod(1:n)      /      (prod(1:2)      *
prod(1:max(n - 2, 1)))
```

The **"explosive roommates function"** is applied first when returning a vector of results. The sapply() function is then used to go through the vector of values x and return a vector of results y. This is demonstrated below in the following examples.

**Step 1:** The vector of the x value is defined.

```
x = 2:20
```

**Step 2:** The sapply() function is used to establish vectors of y values.

```
y                =                sapply(x,
explosive_roommates)
```

**Step 3:** The function plots y against x.

```
qplot(x, y, geom = c("line", "point")) + labs(y
= "Number of potential conflicts", x =
"Number of roommates")
```

```
Note: You can test the above steps
in R to see the results. Make sure
that you declare the "explosive
roommates function" before you enter
them.
```

# Looping

Looping is an advanced concept in R and can be challenge for those who are new to programming. R has looping structures like any other programming language that requires time and effort to master. Looping is a repeated evaluation for a block of statements. The traditional for, while, and repeat loops are used to evaluate statements, but there are other constructs that are used to control the evaluations.

There is an unconventional repeat loop and a family of loops called **"apply"**, **"sapply"**, **"lapply"**, and **"tapply"**. These are used for implicit looping. Traditional loops like for and while loops are used for repetitive actions, but the Apply loop family are used in specific circumstances, such as in ragged arrays. You can also use loops within loops, for example you can use a "while" loop within a "for" loop.

The for, while, and repeat loops are used in R for explicit looping. To control the loops R uses the next and break built-in constructs during an evaluation. The break statement allows you to exit the loop that is currently being executed. The next statement allows you to return to the beginning of the loop to execute the next iteration of the loop. Any statements that are below the statement in this instance will not be evaluated.

After an evaluation, loops will return the value of the last statement that was evaluated. You can also assign the results from the for, while, and repeat statements to a symbol. Looping is not necessary in all operations. You can use vectors that do not require a loop. Values that are returned by loop statements are always NULL, which is not generally noticeable.

Here is some background information that will help you understand how loops work in R:

1. Loops are slow in R. Although they are slow loops will accomplish the task in reasonable time unless you are working with a large dataset. If you are working with lots of data, there ways to get around it.

2. R is written in a C or some variant of C++ type language. When you execute an R code, you are actually executing C code. R uses the underlying C

code to run loops with or without vectors.

3. R provides alternative functions that you can use instead of using loops. The "**apply**" function for example, works faster than the "**for**" loop because it actually has built-in for loop written in R. There are also other functions in the apply family that runs faster than loops. However, a well-constructed loop can run just as fast as apply functions.

When programming in R, you may encounter a problem within a loop. If this happens refer to the following key points:

1. **Reset the set values** – You may have to reset the value or a vector within the loop. It is possible that you may have used a statement within the "**for**" loop that has a value that needs to reset.

2. **Missing brackets** – Sometimes you may have forgotten to put in your square brackets or curly braces within the counter or to the left or right of the statement.

## If/Else Statement

The if/else statement is conditional and evaluates two or more statements. The arguments within the **if'** statement is a logical expression. It is a single block of code, where more blocks can be added after the else statement. It is used to evaluate a logical value. If the value is valid, the first statement is evaluated, and if the first statement is NOT TRUE, then the second statement is evaluated. A value is then returned.

The following is the syntax for the if/else statement:

```
>       if      (       statement1=TRUE)
>                               (result1)
>                                   else
>       result3
```

Here is an example of an "**if/else**" statement.

```
>               x           <-          3
>       if(x    ==    5)    {     print(1)     }
>           else      {          print(2)      }
[1]  2
```

The first "**if**" statement (x == 5) in the above example is evaluated to produce a value. If the value is

TRUE in the first statement, the second statement (print (1)) is evaluated. If the first statement (x==5) is FALSE, the second statement (print(1)) is ignored and the third statement (print(2)) is evaluated. If the value is not logical or valid, an error is returned.

If/else statements are used to prevent numeric problems, such as the logarithm of a negative number. Since if/else statements are the same as other statements you can assign values to them.

In the following "**if/else**" examples, both statements produce the same results.

```
if( any(y <= 1) ) y <- log(1+y)
else x <- log(y)
```

```
x <- if( any(y <= 1) ) log(1+y)
else log(y)
```

The else clause in both examples is optional. Instead, the statement if (any(y<=1)) y <- y[y <= 1] can be used without the else clause. When the "**if**" statement is not within the block and the else is present, you must have the

80

second statement on the same line. If not, the new line at the end of second statement completes the "**if**" statement and returns a complete evaluated statement. The easiest way to resolve this is to insert open and close braces ({ }) for compound statements and by placing the else on the same line as the closing brace (}). The closing brace specifies the end of the statement.

The following '**if/else**" syntax shows how you would nest compound or multiple statements:

```
if ( statement1 )
{ statement2 } else if ( statement3
) { statement4
} else statement6
```

The even numbered statements in the example are evaluated and return a value. If the else clause is ignored and the odd numbered statements return FALSE, then no other statements are evaluated and a NULL value is returned.

The odd numbered statements are evaluated in order until one of them returns TRUE. The even numbered statements are then evaluated. In the above example, statement4 is only evaluated if statement1 returns FALSE.

R allows you to write multiple "**if**" statements in a conditional form. The first statement/expression is evaluated and returns a single logical value. It allows you to use double AND (&&) and OR (‖) operators with the conditional "**if**" statements.

You can use the following operators to produce "**TRUE**" or "**FALSE**", "**T**" or "**F**", "**1**" or "**0**" results in if statements.

- x == y -- This means x is equal to y, for example:

```
if (10 == 5 + 5) print(Yes)
```

- x != y -- This means x is not equal to y, for example:

```
if (10 ! = 5 + 5) print(No)
```

- x > y -- This means x is greater than y, for example:

```
if (10 > 5 ) print(It is greater)
```

- x < y -- This means x is less than y, for example:

```
if (10 < 5) print(It is not greater)
```

- x <= y -- This means x is less than or equal to y, for example:

```
if (10 <= 5 + 5) print (It is equal)
```

- x >= y -- This means x is greater than or equal to y, for example:

```
if (5 >= 10) print (It is less)
```

The **"else"** statement on the other hand is an alternate option. Ideally, the else statement much be written on the same line as the closing brace for the previous **"if"** block.

R provides a vector version for the **"if/else"** statement. It is the **"if/else"** function. The following syntax is used to write the if/else function.

```
ifelse(condition, x, y)
```

This function returns vectors of various lengths and holds the longest argument. It contains the elements x[i] if condition [i] is TRUE, else y[i]. The arguments use vectors of various lengths. The "condition" argument is used to test, x is assessed as a "TRUE" value, and y is assessed a "FALSE" value.

The following example is an **"ifelse"** function that displays 5 vectors.

```
x                    <-                    1:5
ifelse(x<5     |     x>5,     x,     0)
[1]   1  2 4 4 0
```

The ifelse() function takes the first condition, and then takes the second condition if the first is TRUE and the third if the condition is FALSE. The condition can be a vector in this case. In this example, the results show a vector sequence of numbers from 1 to 5. All the values displayed are less than 5 and greater than 5.

## Repeat Statement

The repeat statement is used to repeat an evaluation for a body of statements until a break is implemented. The body of statements is also called a block. Before you use it, you should conduct some calculations and test to determine a break is required from the two statements. When using the repeat statement, you need to be careful because it can cause an infinite loop.

The following syntax is used for the repeat loop:

repeat statement

The repeat statement is frequently used, just like the **"for"** and **"while"** loops. It is used for executing repetitive statements until a condition is met, like with the **"while"** loop. The break statement helps to terminate the repeat loop.

The repeat loop with the break statement looks something like the following syntax:

```
repeat { if (constraint condition)
  {break } }
```

The following information shows how the repeat loop works:

1. The repeat statement uses the **"repeat"** keyword to start the repeat loop.
2. The statements within the curly brackets are the execution statements for the repeat loop.
3. The **"if (constraint condition)"** specifies the constraint condition repeat loop.
4. The break statement inside the repeat loop is used to terminate the repeat loop.
5. When the constraint condition is fulfilled, the code inside the "If" condition checks for the break statement.
6. If the break statement exists, the repeat loop is terminated.

The following example will help you better understand the
repeat loop:

```
>      total      <-     1      repeat
>    {   total    <-    total   +    3;
print(total);
> if (total > 10) break; }
```

This program is designed to repeatedly add 2 to the total
until the required number reaches to 10. In the example,
the total is greater than the 10. The constraint "**total > 10**"
is a constraint condition that is used with the "if" loop. The
"**if**" loop, has a break statement that terminates the repeat
loop when the condition is fulfilled.

The repeat loop has similar functionality to the "**for**" and
"**while**" loops. However, it is used when the user already
knows the constraint conditions and does not want to use
the "**for**" or "**while**" loop because of complexities.

The repeat loop is used like the do/while loop in various
situations in the R language. When you use the repeat
loop, you will notice that it behaves similar to the do/while
loop because it executes statements until the constraint
condition is met.

When implementing the repeat loop, you should consider the following:

1. Ensure that the constraint condition variable for terminating the repeat loop is within the repeat loop.

2. The break statement within the if loop is the only way to terminate the repeat loop.

3. The repeat loop can also be used as a do/while loop.

Bear in mind that the repeat loop is similar to the while loop. However, the repeat loop begins the loop. The while loop on the other hand will only start if the condition is true when it is evaluated the first time. The repeat loop will only terminate the statement if there is break statement. This means that you need to execute the break to come out of the loop. The loop is repeated until the break is specified and requires a second statement to determine whether or not to break from the loop.

## While Loop

The While loop is simple and is one of the best ways to execute repeated statements. The structure is widely used by R programmers, as well as other programmers. It consists of a constraint condition that follows the **"while"** keyword. Following the constraint condition, programming statements are written within the loop brackets. Repetitive conditions are performed until the constraint conditions are met.

The while statement is similar to the repeat statement but uses the following syntax.

```
while        (constraint        condition)
statement1
```

The while statement, **"constraint condition"** is evaluated to test if the value is TRUE. When the **"constraint condition"** is evaluated, **"statement1"** is then evaluated. The evaluation process continues until **"constraint condition"** is evaluated to FALSE. It can be used to repeat a set of instructions when you do not know how the statements will be executed.

The while loop is also similar to the **"for"** loop, but the iterations are controlled by a conditional statement.

The following is an example of a while loop:

```
x                    <-                    0
while(x < 6)

{    x          <-        x        +        1
     print(x)    }
```

The following syntax will further explain the while loop as it is used in R:

```
while (constraint condition)
// while is a keyword; It returns a
true or false value
{      //opening    curly    brackets
//Statements    within    the    curly
brackets
} // closing curly brackets
```

The output or the results of the constraint condition is a Boolean (true or false) value. This Boolean value is controlled by the code that will enter or quit the loop to execute the statement. If the constraint condition is not met, the code control (program) will go within the loop and execute the statements within the loop. An execution within a while loop is considered an iteration. When the iteration is complete, the code control will return to the beginning and reevaluate the constraint condition within the while loop.

A while loop may have multiple statements that may look like the following syntax:

```
while (constraint condition)
```

```
{ statement1;

  statement2;

  statement3; }
```

Here is an explanation of how the while loop works in R:

1. **Initialization** – Initialization of the constraint variable is the first step in the loop. At this point the constraint condition is initialized. It is essential that you initialize the constraint variable before you use it in the while loop. If you do not initialize it, the program may crash or the while loop will go into an indefinite loop because it picks up an invalid value from memory.

2. **Evaluate Constraint Condition and Statements** – The constraint condition within the while loop is responsible for termination. The program evaluates the value of the constraint condition and if the constraint condition is met, the code control goes into the "**while**" loop and execute the statements within the code. While loops are iterated until the condition is met.

3. **Loop Termination** – When the constraint condition is satisfied, the loop is terminated. The code control will stop executing the while loop.

The while loop can get moderately complex. A moderately complex while loop may look similar to the following example:

```
x<-0;

while (x < 5)

{ x<- x+1; print (x); }
```

Here is an explanation of the above example:

1. **x <- 0 (Initialization)** – The statement "x<- 0" shows the initialization of the constraint variable.

2. **x < 5 (Evaluate Condition)** – The statement "x < 5" shows the constraint condition.

3. **x + 1; and print(x) (Evaluate Statements)** - The "x + 1" and "**print(x)**" are the execution statements within the loop.

In the above example, the first iteration evaluates the constraint condition. The constraint condition is not met since x is not initialized to 0. Therefore, the code control will go within the while loop and execute the statements. When the while loop is iterated the third time, the value of x will be 3. When the final iteration occurs, the while loop will terminate.

Sometimes you may not know where to implement a while loop or how to create the right constraint condition because you may not know what the results will look like. In these circumstances, you can set the constraint conditions to "**true**".

The following syntax shows how to set the constraint conditions to "**true**" within a while loop:

```
while                          (true)
{                          statement1;
    statement2;  }
```

The while loop with the constraint condition "true" is also used with for loops. This saves helps with loop performance with dynamically allocated vectors.

Constraint conditions are used to break or terminate the while loop, but it is not the only way. You can also use the break and next statements.

The following example shows how to use the break statement within a while loop.

```
x<-0; while (x < 5)

{       x <- x + 1; print (x);

        if ( x = 4)

{       break;      } }
```

The above example shows that the **"while"** loop will terminate when the value of x is 4. The break statement in the while loop terminates before the constraint condition is met.

Sometimes there are errors with the while loop. They often occur within the constraint conditions. They are semantic and therefore difficult to detect. They may produce false results. To avoid these errors, you must ensure that the constraint variables are performed within the **"while"** loop because they can lead to indefinite execution.

Although the while loop exhibit errors, it is widely accepted by R programmers as an option to execute infinite conditions in real world scenarios.

When implementing the while loop, you should adhere to following key points:

1. Learn the basic concepts of the while loops and how they are implemented in R programming. You

should start off with learning how the **"while"** loop works.

2. Ensure that you initialize the constraint condition variable before executing the while loop. If not, the constraint variable will detect an invalid value from the memory location and create an infinite while loop.

3. Ensure that you have a constraint variable within the while loop to prevent an indefinite execution of the while loop.

4. The while loop is the widely accepted method of executing the infinite loops across various programming languages and in the real world.

5. You can exit the while loop with the constraint condition and break statements.

These key points will help you better understand how the **"while"** loop work and know how to carefully use it.

## For Loop

If you program and develop software applications in other programming languages, you should understand how a for loop works. A for loop in R, is not any different from other for loops in other programming languages. It is used to repeat a set of instructions, but it is also used to help you to know the values a loop variable will have before the loop is executed. The for loop syntax is very simple and looks like the following:

```
for      (variable    in     sequence)
{                            statement1;
   statement2; }
```

The sequence in the above syntax refers to a list or a specific value. For each variable in the sequence, there is a variable name that is set to the value for that element and then statement1 is evaluated. One issue is that the variable name will still exist when the loop is terminated and the value of the last element of the sequence.

For loops can be controlled by a looping vector. Whenever the loop is iterated, a single value is designated in the looping vector and assigned to a variable. The value can be used within the statements of the loop. The number of times the loop is iterated is specified by the values saved in the looping vector. The values are processed in the same order that it is saved in the looping vector.

The for loop can be controversial, but with proper use it will provide results when a specific task is executed a few times. In the following example you will see how the for loop works.

```
val        =        (1,        50,        by=2)
val.squared                =                NULL
for        (i        in        1:25        )        {
val.squared[i] = val[i]^2 }
```

The above example creates a for loop that squares every value of the dataset by using the "**val**" object. It contains the odd integers from 1 to 50. When you create a new vector, you must set up a vector to save into before you execute the loop. In this case, it is "**val.squared = NULL**". An empty vector is created to insert items. It is not the most efficient, but effective. Following the creation of the vector, the "**for**" loop is executed. At this point the for loop will run 25 times(1:25). The counter that is established in this instance is "**i**". This letter is used for the variable name, but you can choose any letter that you would like.

Sometimes you may encounter some problems with the "**for**" loop like putting the right statement within the loop, forgetting to put the subscript in a vector, or missing a bracket on the left or right side. All these and other mistakes are possible. Therefore, before running the "**for**" loop, revisit the constraint condition and the statements within the loop.

If you are writing a for loop within a large program, bear in mind the number of times you would like to loop based on the length of a vector or other factors. In this case set the counter to a specific length. The following example shows a "**for**" loop that designates the number of times based on a specific length.

```
for    (i    in    1:length(val))    {
#statements    that    specifies    the
number of times of the val length. }
```

There are various ways that you can write a "for" loop. it depends on various factors. Here are two key points that will help you create the appropriate for loop within your program.

1. **Limit Statements** - A well constructed loop do not have a lot of "stuff" inside. Try and write most statements outside the loop. If there are any statements or vectors that can be performed outside the loop, put them outside.

2. **Minimize Growing an Object** – Since we are not sure of the results, it is better to use a loop without all the meaningless statements.

You can create condition within a **"for"** loop with an if/else statement. Here is an example of how you would write a for loop with an if/else condition.

```
for(i in seq(along=x)) { if(x[i] <
5)
                                    {
        y <- c(y, x[i] - 1) } else {
        y <- c(y, x[i] / x[i])  } }
y
```

You can also create a stop condition and execute an error message within a **"for"** loop. This is how you would write a for loop that ends a condition and print an error message.

```
for(i     in      seq(along=x))      {
    if (x[i]<5) { y <- c(y,x[i]-1)
    } else { stop("Error:  Values
must be less than <5")} }
```

In the above example, the **"for"** loop shows an example of how you can use a stop statement with an error message within a for loop.

## Switch Statement

The Switch statement is actually a function, but the form is closer to the control structures of programming languages like C and C++. It typically evaluates an expression and returns a value in a list, based on the same index. The results are based on the data type of the expression.

The basic syntax for the switch statement looks like the following:

```
switch (statement, list);
```

Here is also another way that you can view the switch syntax:

```
switch(statement,                 item1
,item2,item3,...,itemN).
```

The first thing that happens within the switch statement is the evaluation of the **"statement"** to produce results. The elements within the list are named.

Here is an example of how you will write the switch statement:

```
x <- as.integer(2) > x [1] 2 >
```

```
z = switch(x,1,2,3,4,5) > z [1] 2 >
x <- 3.5 >
z = switch(x,1,2,3,4,5) > z [1] 3
```

The expression within the switch statement is viewed as an integer, if it is not an integer. If the result of the expression on the other hand is a string, then the items in the list will have the form "**valueN = resultN**".

The switch statements can be fairly basic, but can also be complex. The following example shows a more complex switch statement.

```
switch(6,     2+2,     mean(1:10),
rnorm(5))

      NULL
```

The above switch statement evaluates a value that is s between 1 and 10. The element relating to the list is then evaluated and a result is returned. If the value is too small or large, NULL is returned. In this case, the value is too large. This means that the value was not specified and no match was found.

Another way to use the switch statement is produce results

according to the character value of one of the arguments within the function.

Here is how you can create a switch statement based on a character value.

```
> y <- "furniture"
> switch(y, furniture = "bed",
appliance = "radio", "Neither")
[1] "bed"
```

The above example produces the final result by taking the object "**y**" and evaluating its value within the switch statement. It compared the value of "**y**" with list to determine the correct character value, which is "**bed**".

## Break and Next Statements

The "**break**" statement is used to terminate loops. This is actually the only way to terminate repeat loops. The execution of the current loop is stopped and exited.

The "**next**" statement on the other hand is for discontinuing a specific sequence and the skip to the next one. It is used to skip the following statements and restart the current loop. When a for loop is present, the next statement will perform an update of the loop variable.

Here is an example of how the break and next statement is used within a "**for**" loop and if condition. T

```
> for(myloop in x)   {    if (myloop >
2.0)     next   if(   (myloop<0.6)   &&
(myloop > 0.5))

> break cat("The value of my loop is
",myloop,"\n");   }

   The value of my loop is 1.416993

   The   value  of  my  loop  is    -
0.01571884
```

In the above example the next and the break statements are implemented within the "for" loop. There is also a conditional if statement inside the "**for**" loop. You can test the break and next statements with any for loop. Just ensure that you follow the proper structure.

## Apply Loop Family

The Apply Loop family is alternative to writing traditional loops like the for and while loops. While and for loops are easy to write but can be tedious and quite difficult to write on the command line. Therefore, R provides some functions that allow you to implement loops to make it easier. These functions have built in for loops written in R.

These functions are under the apply loop family category. They are apply, lapply, sapply, and tapply loops.

Here is some additional information about the apply loops:

1. **apply loop**: The "**apply**" loop is used to process array margins.
2. **lapply loop**: The "**lapply**" loop is for a list and to evaluate a function with elements.
3. **sapply loop**: The "**sapply**" is similar to the lapply and it is used to enhance results in simple formats.

4. **tapply loop**: The "**tapply**" loop is a function used for processing vector subsets.

In following sections, you will learn more about the apply loops through examples.

## Apply Loop

The apply loop is for evaluating anonymous functions over the array margins, but it is mostly used to apply a loop for matrix columns and rows. They can also be used over the arrays. This means that it can be used to calculate the average of matrices arrays. It is not necessarily faster than a traditional loop, but it can be written on just one line.

The apply loop is actually a function, and basically can be written as a function. The following example shows how you can write the apply loop as a function:

```
str                              (apply)
function (A, NUM, FUNCTION, ...)
```

In the above example, the arguments are explained as follows:

- "**A**" is used to represent an array.

- "**NUM**" is used to represent an integer vector for the required margin.

- **"FUNCTION"** is the function or function name to apply.
- **". . ."** refers to additional arguments that will be passed within the **"FUNCTION"**.

To better understand the apply loop, here two examples to show you how you can use the apply loop.

1. **Find Mean Values:** The apply loop shows how to measure the mean values of a matrix that is stored in x.

```
> x <- matrix (rnorm (100), 10, 5)
> apply (x, 2, mean)
```

2. **Summation of Matrix:** The following example shows how to calculate the summation of a matrix stored in x.

```
> x <- matrix (rnorm (100), 10, 5)
> apply(x, 1, sum)
```

You can enter the commands in the command line of the R program to see the results.

## Lapply Loop

The next loop to be discussed in the apply loop family is the **"lapply"** loop. The lapply loop is specified for lists.

This means that it is used to evaluate the elements within a list.

Here is the syntax for the lapply loop:

```
>                                    lapply
> function (A, FUNCTION, ...)
```

```
> { FUNCTION <- sport.fun (FUNCTION)
> if (!is.vector(A) || is.object(A))
> A <- as.list(x).Internal(lapply(A,
FUN)) }
```

As previously mentioned, most of the code that belongs to R comes from the C language and the actual loop for the lapply was coded in C. Therefore, the output created looks similar to the results that you will see in C. The "**lapply**" outputs its results in a list, regardless of the input class used.

Here is are two examples of how the "**lapply**" functionality works:

1. **Extract Mean Values:** The lapply is used in the following example to extract the mean values from the list that holds the x variable. The output will always be in a list format.

```
> x <- list(i = 1:5, n = rnorm(10))
> lapply (x, mean)
```

2. **Count Characters:** In the following example, the lapply is used to count the character for each string.

```
> x <- c("fruit", "veg", "i",
"plant")
> lapply (x, nchar)
```

3. **Extract Columns:** The lapply is used here to extract the first column from a matrix.

```
> lapply (y, function(abc) abc[,1])
```

The lapply examples above can be tested in the command line of the R program. Test them to see the results.

## Sapply Loop

The sapply is the next loop in the apply loop family that you will learn more about. As previously mentioned, it is used to simplify the output. If the result is in a list form with an element of length 1 for each, then the sapply will attempt to return the output in a vector form.

The sapply syntax looks like the following:

```
>                              sapply
> function (A, FUNCTION, ...)
```

The following example shows how the sapply function is used to create the output of a string. To better understand the sapply function, the following example you will see how it .

```
> x <- c("fruit", "veg", "i",
"plant")
> sapply(x, nchar)
```

The output for the above example would look like the following:

```
fruit veg  i  plant
  5      3  1    5
```

## Tapply Loop

The tapply is the last loop in the apply family. As you previously learned, it is used to process the vector subsets. It is also used with arrays that have variable lengths. The grouping of the tapply loop is specified by the factor.

The following syntax defines the tapply loop:

```
>                       str(tapply)
> function (V, FACTOR, FUNCTION =
NULL, ..., simple = TRUE)
```

108

Here is an explanation of the arguments within the function:

- **V** – This is the vector.
- **FACTOR** – This is the list of factor or a single factor.
- **FUNCTION** – This is the function that was previously used.
- **...** – This specifies the arguments for the function.
- **Simple** – This determines if the simplified results are necessary.

Here are some examples of the tapply loop:

```
> x <- a(rnorm(5), runif(5),
rnorm(5,                    1))
> b <- gl(3,    5)
> f
```

```
> tapply(y, b, mean)
```

```
> tapply(y, b, mean, simplify =
FALSE)
```

Here are some valuable key points that you should consider when implementing the Apply Loop family:

1. The loops in the apply loop family represents functions implemented as loops.

2. The apply loop family helps programmers avoid writing complex loops at the command line.

3. Using a specific loop in the apply loop family is based on the variable used for input.

## Using Tapply() Function

R uses the tapply() function for various calculations, such as calculating the mean, calculating standard errors, and calculating vectors. Vectors that are combined are called ragged arrays.

The following examples will show you how to use the tapply() function to perform different calculations:

- **Mean Calculation:** The tapply() function can be used to calculate the mean income for example. The following example calculates the mean income.

```
> incmeans <- tapply(incomes,
statef, mean)
```

The tapply() is used to apply a function with the **"mean()"** function for each group of components. Within the function **"incomes"** and **"statef"** are implemented as if they are separate vector structures. The result has the structure with the same length as the levels attribute for the factor.

- **Calculate Standard Errors** – You can write an R function to calculate the standard errors for any vector. R has a built-in function called var() for calculating the sample variance. This is a very simple one-line function. The following example shows how to assign the var() and then use the tapply() function to calculate the errors. Here is how you could assign the var() function and use the tapply() function to calculate standard errors:

```
>        stderr        <-        function(x)
sqrt(var(x)/length(x))
```

You can also use the tapply() function to find the confidence limits for a state's mean income, for example. In this case, you would use the tapply() function with the length() function to determine the sample sizes and the qt() function to calculate the percentage points of the t-distributions.

Additionally, the tapply() function is capable of handling complex indexing for vectors within various categories. You can use it to separate the tax accountants by state and sex. In this instance, the values of the vector are collected in groups relating to the entries. The tapply() function is applied to each group, individually. The results would be a vector with the levels attribute label.

When the vector and the labeling factor are combined, it is called a ragged array because the subclass sizes are irregular. If the subclass sizes are the same, the indexing is done implicitly and more efficiently.

## Sequences

There are various accommodations within R for creating popular sequences. You could have 1:20 that represents the vector v(1,2, 3, ... 19,20). The colon operator is considered top priority for the expression. If the you have 2*1:10 for the vector v(2, 4, 6, ..., 18, 20), you could put n <- 10 and compare the sequences 1:n-1 and 1(n-1). You may also create a backward sequence using the construction 20:1. This means the result would be a backward sequence.

R also uses the function "seq()" normally to create sequences. The function carries five arguments, but only some of them can be defined with one call. If the two first arguments are provided, they would specify the beginning and the end of the sequence. If these are the only two arguments within the function, then the result is the same as the colons. If the sequence function is defined as seq(2:20), then it is the same vector as 2:20.

The arguments for the seq() function and other R function are also defined in name form. This means that the order of appearance is irrelevant. The first two arguments in the function could have **"from=value"** and **"to=value"**. Therefore seq(1,20), seq(from=1, to=20, and seq(to=30, from=1) means the same as 1:20. The following two arguments relating to the seq() function can be by=value and length=value. This means a step size and the length of the sequence separately. If none of these are given, then by=1 is assumed by default.

The following examples show how the seq() function is create a sequence of vectors and other operations:

```
> seq1 <- seq(-3, 3, by=.2)
```

- This example has three arguments with the vector v(-3.0, -2.8, -2.6, ...., 2.6, 2.8, 3.0) stored in seq1.

```
> seq2 <- (length=31, from=-3,
by=.2)
```

113

- This example is similar to the above, but generate the vector in seq2. The third argument may also be called along=vector. This is typically used as a single argument to create the sequence 1, 2, 3, … length(vector) or have an empty sequence if the vector is empty.

There is also another function that is similar to the seq() function. The rep() function is used for duplicating an object in complex ways.

The simplest form for the rep() function may look like the following:

```
> s3 <- rep(x, qty=3)
```

- This example will put three copies of x into s3.

There is also another version that you can use that looks like the following:

```
> s4 <- rep(x, each=3)
```

- This example repeats each element about three times before going to the next.

## Sequence Generation

To help you better understand sequences, you will learn

some addition details about sequence generation in this section, such as usage and arguments used.

The seq() function is standard generic sequence which is a default method. However, there are derivatives that are faster and have fewer restrictions. These include "**seq.int**", "**seq_along**", and "**seq_len**" functions.

The sequence function provides different formats to manipulate and calculate different data types.

The sequence function uses the following syntaxes:

```
seq(...)     // This is the default
method.
```

```
seq(from = 1, to = 1, by = ((to -
from)/(length.out - 1)), length.out
= NULL, along.with = NULL, ...)
```

```
seq.int(from, to, by, length.out,
along.with, ...)
```

```
seq_along(along.with)
seq_len(length.out)
```

Here is an explanation of the arguments used inside the seq, seq.int(), and seq_along() functions above.

- **...** - This is used inside the seq() and seq.int() functions are arguments passed to or from methods.

- **from, to** – The "**from, to**" argument in the seq() and seq.int() functions is the starting and greatest end values of the sequence. It is length 1 unless "from" is only used as an unnamed argument.

- **by** – The "**by**" argument in the seq() and seq.int() functions is used to set the number of increments for the sequence.

- **length.out** – The "**length.out**" argument in the seq(), seq.int(), and seq.along() functions is the desired length of the sequence. It is a positive number and in the case of the seq and seq.int functions will be rounded up if it is a fraction.

- **along.with** - The "**along.with**" argument has the length of the length of the argument.

Here is some additional details about the arguments inside the seq() functions:

- **from** – This is the starting value of the sequence.

- **to** – This is the maximal or greatest end value of the sequence.

- **by** – This is the increment of the sequence.

- **length.out** – This is the desired length of the sequence.

- **along.with** – This is the length starting from the length of the current argument.

- **a, b** – These are factors with the same length.

**Additional Details**

The input numbers should always be finite. This means that the numbers that you use must not be infinite, NaN(Not a Number) or NA. The unnamed arguments for the seq() and seq.int() are not standard, therefore it is recommended that you always name your arguments when you are programming.

- **Seq()** - The seq() function is generic, as previously mentioned, therefore it dispatches on the class of the first argument regardless of the names of the arguments. This can have unintentional consequences if it is called with only a single argument when used with the along.with() function. Instead, it is better to use the seq_along() function.

- **seq.int()** – The seq.int() function is an internally generic function for the seq() function based on the class for the first given argument.

The seq() function have different usages. The typical usages include the following:

- **seq(from, to)** – The "**seq(from,to)**" function creates the sequence "from", "from +/-1", ... to. This is the same as from:to.

```
seq(1,10)
```

- **seq(from, to, by=)** – The "**seq(from,to,by=)**" creates from, from+/-1, ... up to the sequence number that is less than or equal to "to". When you specify to, from, and by with opposite signs is incorrect. The calculated value may go above the "to", to allow a rounding error, but it is truncated to the "to".

```
seq(1, 6, by = pi)
```

- **seq(from, to, length.out=)** – The "**seq(from, to, length.out=)**" format creates a length.out sequence that has equal values from "from" to "to". The length.out argument normally is abbreviated from length to len. It is actually faster to write seq_len.

- **seq(along.with=)** – The "**seq(along.with=)**" format creates the integer sequence of 1, 2, 3, ..... length(along.with). The along.width is typically abbreviated to along. It is actually faster to write seq_along.

```
seq(stats::rnorm(20)))
```

- **seq(from)** – The "**seq(from)**" format creates the sequence 1, 2, 3, …. length(from). It acts as if the argument along.with is defined. When the argument.

```
seq(17)
```

- **seq(length.out)** – The "**seq(length.out)**" format creates the integer sequence 1, 2, 3, … length.out=0, when it generates integer(0).

```
seq(0, 1, length.out = 11)
```

```
Note: The seq.int() and the default
seq()     function    with    numeric
arguments will return an integer or
double vector. The seq_along() and
seq_len() functions will return an
integer vector, unless the vector is
of type long.
```

# Data Manipulation

R uses objects to generate and manipulate variables, array of numbers, functions, characters, and other structures. When in an R session, R creates objects and store them with a name. The command may look like the following syntaxes.

```
objects()
```

or

```
Is()
```

The Is() function can be used to display most of the names for the objects stored in R. The collection of objects is known as workspace. If you would like to remove any of the objects, the "**rm()**" function can be used.

Here is an example of how you would use the "**rm()**" function.

```
> rm(a, b, c, res, temp, num, com
```

All the objects stored in an R session is permanently stored for future use. When the session ends, you have the option of saving all the objects that are currently available. When you confirm this option, the objects are saved in the .RData file within the current directory. The command lines that are used in the session are saved in the ".Rhistory" file. When R is restarted from the same directory, the workspace reloads from the file. The commands used previously will also reload.

When you are doing analyses, it is recommended that you use different working directories. Objects with x and y names are commonly created during these analyses. The names are worthwhile, but can be difficult to determine the time the analyses are conducted within the same directory.

## Data Structures

R uses named data structures, such as numeric vectors. A numeric vector is a single entity that contains a collection of ordered numbers. If you would like to create a vector with the name y that contains five numbers, namely 2.4, 3.5, 4.7, 1.3, and 20.8, R you would use the following statement:

```
> y <- v(2.4, 3.5, 4.7, 1.3, 20.8)
```

This v() function in the above example is assigned to the y variable. The function used in this context takes any random number with the vector arguments and have a vector value that was obtained through concatenating the arguments. The number that occurs independently in a statement has the vector length of one.

The assignment operator (<-) in the above example contains two characters, the less than (<) and minus (-) signs that are close together. It is a short cut for creating assignments. It points to the object that is storing the expression or statement. As mentioned earlier, the equal sign(=) can be used as an alternative in most cases. You may also use the assign() function to assign functions to variables.

Here is how you would use the assign() function to perform an assignment:

```
> assign("y", v(2.4, 3.5, 4.7, 1.3,
20.8))
```

Earlier, it was also noted that assignments can be made in the opposite direction. You only need to put the variable to the right and switch the position of the assignment operator.

This is how you would create an assignment in the opposite direction:

```
> v(2.4, 3.5, 4.7, 1.3, 20.8 ) -> y
```

When an expression is a complete statement, the value is printed and lost. If you use the following statement, the reciprocals for the five values would be printed to the command line and the value of y would not change.

```
1/yt
```

## Vector Manipulation

R uses vectors in arithmetic expressions, where the operations are performed an element at a time. The vectors inside the same expression do not have to have the same length. When the length is not the same, then the value of the expression would have the same length as the longest vector of the expression. Shorter vectors on the other hand are recycled until a match for the longest vector is found.

In the following example, the vector x contains 11 entries that contains 2 copies of y and 0.

```
x <- v(y, 0, y)
```

In the above assignment, you can use the following statement to generate a new vector with the length of 11.

```
v <- 2*x+y+1
```

The above example is constructed by adding each element

at a time. The statement 2 * x is repeated 2.2 times, y is repeated once and 1 is repeated 11 times. Other commonly used arithmetic functions such as log, exp, sin, cos, tan, and sqrt can also be used to calculate vectors in R. They all have different meanings.

- **max()** - The max() function selects the largest vector or arguments, even with several arguments. A similar function is the pmax() function which returns a vector that is equal to the vector. It contains the largest element of any input vector.

- **min()** – The min() function selects the smallest vector or arguments, even with several arguments. A similar function is the pmin() function which returns a vector that is equal to the vector. It contains the smallest element of any input vector.

- **range()** – The range() function has a vector value of length two, namely c(min(x), max(x), max(x))

- **length(x)** – The length() function is number of elements in x.

- **sum(x)** – The sum() function provides the total element for x.

- **prod(x)** – The prod() function provides the product

for x.

- **sort(x)** – The sort() function returns a vector with the same size as x. The elements are arranged in increasing order, but there are also other more flexible sorting options with the order() and sort.list() functions. They production a variation for sorting elements.

R also provides two statistical functions. They are:

- **mean(x)** – This calculates the sample mean. It is the same as sum(x)/length(x).

- **var(x)** – This results in results in sum((x-mean(x))^2/length(x)-1) or sample variance. If the argument for var() is an n-by-p matrix, then the value is a p-by-p sample that the covariance matrix received with regard to the rows as independent p-variant sample vectors.

In most cases, users are not concerned with the data type of the numeric vector. If a numeric vector is an integer, real or complex, the internal calculations are calculated as double precision real numbers or double precision complex numbers(if the input data is complex).

If you are working with complex numbers, provide an explicit complex solution, like the one used in the following example:

```
sqrt(-17+0i)
```

The above example will compute complex numbers, but if you use the following example, you will receive a NaN (Not a Number) warning.

```
sqrt(-17)
```

## Object Manipulation

R uses three types of language objects for modifications; expressions, calls, and functions. However, in this ebook you will learn about call objects. Call objects are also called "unevaluated expressions". The best way to obtain a call object is by using the quote() function with an expression argument.

The following examples use the quote() function with expression arguments:

```
> obj1 <- quote(2 + 2)
> obj2 <- quote(plot(x, y))
```

The arguments are not evaluated, but the results are parsed arguments. In the above example, obj1 and obj2 can also be evaluated with using eval or just be manipulated as data. Obviously, obj2 uses "call" because a call is made to the plot function with the x and y arguments. The "obj1" object also uses the same structure as a call to the binary operator along with two arguments.

This following example explains the structure:

```
> quote("+"(2, 2)) 2+2
```

The contents of the call object are accessed with a list type syntax, which can be convert to and from lists with the "**as.list**" and "**as.call**". When the keyword argument matching is used in the following ways, the keywords can be used as list tags:

```
> obj3 <- quote(plot(x = age, y =
weight))
>                                obj3$x
  age
```

```
> obj3$y weight
```

The contents of the call object have the "name" mode, based on the previous example. The identifiers in the calls are true, but the contents within the call are constants. Constants can be of any type, but the first content must be a function if the call is successfully evaluated.

Objects with the mode name maybe created from character strings using as.name.

This is how you would modify the obj2 using as.name:

```
obj2[[1]] <- as.name("+")  > obj2x+y
```

The following example shows that subexpressions are actually calls:

```
> obj1[[2]] <- obj2 > obj1x+y+2
```

The grouped parentheses inputted are saved in parsed expressions. They represent functions with one argument, therefore $4 - (2-2)$ results in "-"(4, "(" ("-"(2, 2))) in prefix notation. The open brace ('(') operator in this case returns an argument. This can be an issue, but it can be challenging to write a parser/deparser that saves the user input, store it minimally, and ensure that parsing the deparsed expression returns the same expression.

Noticeably, the parser in R is not really invertible or the deparser as the following examples will show:

```
> 						str(quote(c(1,2)))
  language c(1, 2)
```

```
> 						str(c(1,2))
  val [1:2] 1 2
```

```
> 					deparse(quote(c(1,2)))
  [1] "c(1, 2)"
```

```
> 					deparse(c(1,2))
[1] "c(1, 2)"
```

```
> 		quote("-"(2, 			2)) 			2-2
> quote(2 - 2) 2-2
```

Deparsed expressions should evaluate to equal values to the original expression.

The internal part of an expression does not need modifications regularly. However, the user may want to get an expression to deparse and use it for labeling plots.

Here is example of how this can be done:

```
> xlabel     <-    if    (!missing(x))
> deparse(substitute(x))
```

In the above example the variable or expression with the x argument will be used for labeling the x axis. The substitute() function is used to achieve this. It takes the x expression and substitutes the expression that was passed previously with the x argument. This will happen when x carries the information about the expression creating the value.

A formal argument intends for an object to have the following three slots:

1. A slot for the expression that defines the object.
2. A slot for the environment to evaluate the expression.
3. A slot for the value for the expression that was already evaluated.

If a substitute was invoked within the function, the local variable will also be open to substitution. The substitution argument does not necessarily have to be a simple identifier. Instead it can be an expression that involves several variables and substitutions. The substitute function also has an additional argument that can be an environment or a list. The following example shows how this works.

```
>   substitute(x + y, list(x = 1, y =
quote(a)))  1+a
```

In the above example, quoting is used to substitute x. This example works well in circumstances where math expressions are required to create graphs, as shown in the following example:

```
>                                        plot(0)
>          for        (i        in        1:4)
+                  text(1,      0.2      *      i,
+       substitute(x[ix]  ==  y, list(ix =
i, y = pnorm(i))))
```

The substitutions are purely verbiage and there is no testing to see if the call objects make sense when they are evaluated. The substitute(x <- x + 1, list(x=2)) will return 2 <- 2 + 1. It is important to note that R sets its own rules and execute expressions based on what makes sense. If an expression does not make sense, R might still some use for them. Using some mathematical expressions in graphs for example may involve some constructions that are constructed correctly, however can be meaningless when it is evaluated, for example, "{} >= 20 * "years"".

Substitute does not evaluate the first argument, which can be confusing when you are substituting an object within a variable. To resolve this issue, you should use the substitute() function more than once.

The following example shows how to use the substitute() function more than once:

```
> expr <- quote(x + y)
> substitute(substitute(y, list(x =
2)),        list(y       =        expr))
> substitute(x + y, list(x = 2))
>        eval(substitute(substitute(y,
list(x = 2)), list(y = expr))) 2+z
```

R provides the following rules for substitutions:

- In each symbol of the parse tree, the first one corresponds with second. It can be a tagged list or an environment frame.

- A simplified local object inserts a value; otherwise it corresponds to the global environment.

- The expression of a potential function argument is substituted.

- When the symbol does not correspond, it is not used.

- The special exception at a higher level is different because it was inherited from the S language. Therefore, there no control over which variables would be bound at this level and it is better to make substitute behave like a quote.

The rule relating to the potential substitution is a little different from the one used in the S language when the local variable is modified before the substitution. In this case, R will use the new value of the variable. S however will unconditionally use the argument within the expression (unless it was used as constant). This means that f(1) in R maybe completely different from f(1) used in S. The usage in R is cleaner.

Consider the following code to get a better understanding of the substitution:

```
plotlog    <-    function(x,    xlab    =
deparse(substitute(x)))

{         x <- log(x)

          plot(x, xlab = xlab) }
```

This may seem clear, but actually the x label becomes a

poor expression. This occurs because the "lazy evaluation" rule causes the "xlab" expression to happen after x is modified. The solution is to ensure the "xlab" expression is evaluated first.

The following example shows how to evaluate the "**xlab**" expression first:

```
plotlog  <-   function(x,   xlab  =
deparse(substitute(x)))

{   xlab

    x              <-           log(x)
         plot(x, xlab = xlab)       }
```

You will notice in the above example that eval(xlab) is not used. If xlab is a language or an expression object, then the object will be evaluated as well.

The R variant for the substitute() is the bquote() function. It is used to replace some subexpressions with values. The following examples show how to replace the substitute() function with the bquote() function. The syntax for the bquote() function is actually borrowed from the List

Processing (LISP) program back quote macro.

```
// The substitute() function is used
here!
>                       plot(0)
>        for      (i     in      1:4)
> text(1, 0.2 * i, substitute(x[ix]
== y, list(ix = i, y = pnorm(i))))
```

```
// The bquote() function is used
instead     of    the    substitute()
function.
>                       plot(0)
>         for(i          in       1:4)
> text(1, 0.2*i, bquote( x[.(i)]  ==
.(pnorm(i)) ))
```

In the above example, the expression used in the bquote()
function is quoted except the contents within the
subexpressions, which are replaced with its values.

## Function Manipulation

You will know how a function is called just by looking at
the "**sys.call()**" function. The following example shows
how the sys.call() function is used to return its own call.

```
> f <- function(x, y, ...)
sys.call()
> f(y = 1, 2, z = 3, 4)
> f(y = 1, 2, z = 3, 4)
```

The sys.call() function is not necessarily useful unless it is being used for debugging because it requires the function to track the corresponding argument to interpret the call. For example, it must ensure that the second argument corresponds to the first one. This would be the x argument in the above example.

Frequently, the user requires that the call have all the arguments bound to the corresponding formal arguments. To establish this, the match.call() function is used instead of the sys.call() function.

```
> f <- function(x, y, ...)
match.call()
> f(y = 1, 2, z = 3, 4)
> f(x = 2, y = 1, z = 3, 4)
```

In the above example, you will notice that the second argument x corresponds to y, which is displayed in the result. This technique is primarily used to call another function with the same arguments and potentially deleting other functions.

136

The match.call() function uses an expand.dots argument to collect single argument when it is set to FALSE. The following example shows how the **"expand.dots"** argument.

```
> f <- function(x, y, ...)
match.call(expand.dots = FALSE)
> f(y = 1, 2, z = 3, 4)
> f(x = 2, y = 1, ... = list(z = 3,
4))
```

The '...' argument within the function is a list. It is best to use this form of the match.call() function so you do not have to pass undefined argument to functions that will not recognize them.

R provides the call and do.call functions for constructing function calls. The call() function allows you to create a call object from the function with a list of arguments. The following example implements the call() function:

```
> y <- 5.5
> call("round", y)
> round(5.5)
```

You can see that the value of y is inserted in the call instead of the symbol. Therefore, it is definitely different from round(y). This method is rarely used, but sometimes it is useful when the name of a function is available as a character.

The do.call() function is related to the call() function, but it immediately evaluates the call and uses the arguments from an object with the arguments. You can use it to apply function such as the cbind to elements of a **"list"** or a data frame.

The following example shows the implementation of the cbind argument in the do.call() function.

```
> is.na.data.frame <- function (y)
> {   y <- do.call("cbind", lapply(y,
"is.na"))
> rownames(x) <- row.names(y)   x}
```

There are other variations of the do.call() function. It looks like do.call("f", list(...)). This variation requires some evaluation of the arguments before the call is made. This is the downside to "lazy substitution" and argument substitution within the function. A similar concept also relates to the call() function.

R provides a useful way for manipulating the components of a function or a closure. A group of interface functions is used to achieve this goal.

The following details explain the contents of the interface functions:

- **body** – The body returns the expression that is within the body of the function. It also sets the body of the function to an expression that is already provided.

- **formal arguments** – The formal arguments is a list within the function. This is called a **"pair list"**. It also sets the formal arguments of the argument to a provided list.

- **environment** – The environment related to the function is returned. It also sets the environment for the function. The bindings can also be changed for different variables within the environment of the function.

  You can accomplish this by using the evalq() function:

```
> evalq(x <- 5, environment(f)).
```

The as.list() function may also be used to convert a

function to a list. This results in a concatenation of the list of the formal arguments within the body of the function. The list can also be converted to a function using the as.function. This is mainly used for compatibility with S. Apparently, the as.list() function is lost within the environment, but the as.function provides an argument that sets the environment.

## Subsetting

R provides operators for subsetting that are fast and powerful. R allows you to use subsetting to clearly express complex operations better than other languages.

Although subsetting is challenging, it is necessary when you would like to develop the following related concepts:

- The three subsetting operators.
- The six different types of subsetting.
- Key differences relating to the behavior of objects, such as vectors, data frames, lists, factors and matrices.
- Using subsetting with assignments.

In this section you will learn about subsetting. You will start by leaning the simple concepts and then you will gradually learn about advance concepts. You will learn concepts like subsetting an atomic with the open bracket ([), complicated data types (arrays and lists), and subsetting operators (double

140

brackets ([[) and dollar operator($) ). Later on, you will learn about combining subsetting and assignments. You will also learn about modifying objects.

Subsetting uses the str() function to show the structure of an object. It allows you to separate the contents that work best for you.

## Subsetting Data Types

There are six different data types that are used to subset atomic vectors in R. They are used to subset lists, S3 objects, data frames, and matrices.

In the following example, a simple vector x will show the basic concept of subsetting:

```
> x <- c(3.2, 2.2, 3.3, 6.4)
```

In this example the number after the decimal point provides the original position within the vector. This example will be used to explain the different data types used for subsetting a vector.

The following examples details the six different data types used for subsetting a vector:

1. **Positive integers** – Positive integers return elements at specified positions, for example:

```
>                    x[2,              4]
[1] 2.2 6.4
```

```
// This duplicates the indices and
return       duplicated       values.
>               x[c(1,              1)]
[1] 3.2 3.2
```

```
//Real  numbers  or  decimals  are
discretely  truncated  to  integers.
> x[c(2.3, 2.7)]

[1] 2.2 2.2 6.4
```

2. **Negative integers** – Negative numbers are used to skip elements at specified positions, for example:

```
>                    x[-c(3,            1]
[1] 2.2 6.4
```

You can also use them to skip elements, as shown in the following examples:

```
// This first element is skipped.
>                              x[-1]
 [1]2.2
```

```
// The first and second element is
skipped.
>                  x[-c(1,          2)]
[1] 3.3 6.4
```

> **Note:** You cannot mix positive integers in single subsets. This will return an error.

The following example shows an error resulting from a mixed integer subset.

```
// An error is returned because
negative and positive numbers should
not be mixed in a subset.
>                  x[c(-3,          1)]
Error in x[c(-3, 1)]: only 0's may
be mixed with negative subscripts
```

3. **Logical vectors** – Logical vectors allows you to select elements for logical values that are "TRUE". This is considered to be the most useful form of subsetting because the expression is written to create the logical vector.

   The following example shows the concept of logical vectors:

```
// Only the first two decimals are
returned.
> x[c(TRUE, TRUE, FALSE, FALSE)]
[1] 3.2 2.2
```

```
// Only the decimals greater than 3
is                              returned.
>           x[x         >         3]
[1] 3.2 3.3 6.4
```

When the logical vector is shorter than the subsetted vector, it will produce the same length.

```
>              x[c(TRUE,        FALSE)]
[1] 3.2 3.3
```

This example is also the same as the following:

```
> x[c(TRUE, FALSE, TRUE, FALSE)
[1] 3.2 3.3
```

When a value is missing in the index, the results will show a missing value, like the one in the following example:

```
>x[c(TRUE, TRUE, NA, FALSE)]

[1] 3.2 2.2  NA
```

4. **Nothing** – Nothing returns the original vector. This is helpful for matrices, data frames, and arrays, but

144

not for vectors. You can also use it with assignments.

```
> []

[1] 3.2 2.2 3.3 6.4
```

5. **Zero** – Zero returns a vector with zero-length. This is not done intentionally, but you can use it create test data.

Here is an example of how zero subsetting is implemented:

```
> x[0]
```

6. **Character Vectors** – Character vectors are used when a vector is a name. They return elements with matching names. The following examples show how character vectors are used in subsetting.

```
> y <- setNames(x, letters[1:4])
[1]  a       b       c       d
[2] 3.2  2.2  3.3  6.4
```

```
//Indices are repeated just like
integers
>        y[c]"b",      "b",      "b")]
[1]   b           b           b
[2]2.2 2.2 2.2
```

```
// The open brackets ([) are matched
> z <- c(abc = 1, def = 2)
>               z[c("a",           "d")]
[1]              <NA>              <NA>
[2]  NA  NA
```

As previously mentioned, data types are used to subset lists, S3 objects, data frames, and matrices.

R also provides powerful indexing features to help you access object elements. They can be used to choose or omit specific variables and observations. In the following code, you will see various ways you can retain or remove variables and observations so you can take random samples from a dataset.

### 1. Selecting Variables

```
// select variables s1, s2, s3
> mysamples <- c("s1", "s2", "s3")
> newsample <- myinfo[mysamples]
```

```
// Here us another example of
another                      method
> mysamples <- paste("s", 1:3,
sep="")
> newsample <- myinfo[mysamples]
```

```
// Selecting the first and fifth
variables through the tenth variable
> newsample <- myinfo[c(1,5:10)]
```

## 2. Removing Variables

The following examples show how to remove variables:

```
// Variables s1, s2, s3 are omitted.
> mysamples <- names(myinfo) %in%
c("s1",       "s2",       "s3")
> newsample <- myinfo[!mysamples]
```

```
//The 3rd and 5th variables are
omitted.
> newsample <- myinfo[c(-3,-5)]
// Variables s3 and s5 is deleted
> myinfo$s3 <- myinfo$s5 <- NULL
```

## 3. Selecting Observations

The following examples show how to select observations:

```
// The first 5 observations are
selected.
> newsample <- myinfo[1:5,]
```

147

```
// Variable values are selected
> newsample <- myinfo[
which(myinfo$gender=='F'
> & myinfo$age > 65), ]
```

```
// Alternate code for selecting
variable values
> attach(newinfo)
> newsample <- myinfo[
which(gender=='F' & age > 65),]
> detach(newsample)
```

## 4. Subset Function

The "**subset()**" function is one of the easiest ways to select variables. The following example will show you how it is used to select rows with a value ("**ages**") greater than or equal to 30 or less than 20. The "**ID**" and "**Height**" columns are retained.

```
// The subset() function is used
> newsample <- subset(myinfo, age >=
30 | age < 20,
> select=c(ID, Height))
```

In the following example, a group of men over the age of 30 is selected. The height and salary variables are kept, along with all the other columns in between.

```
// The subset() function is used to
select        specific        columns
>   newsample   <-   subset(myinfo,
sex=="m"    &    age    >    30,
> select=height:salary)
```

## 5. Selecting Random Samples

The sample() function allows you to take a random sample of a specific size from a dataset.

```
// The sample() function takes a
random sample of size 40 from the
dataset                    myinfo
// The sample does not have a
replacement
>           mysample          <-
myinfo[sample(1:nrow(myinfo),   40,
> replace=FALSE),]
```

## Subset Lists

Subsetting a list is similar to subsetting an atomic vector, where the open bracket "[" always returns a list, the double open brackets "[[" and the dollar operator "$" allows you to remove the components from the list.

## Matrices and Arrays

The following three ways are used to subset higher-dimensional structures:

1. Subset with multiple vectors.
2. Subset with a single vector.
3. Subset with a matrix.

The most commonly used method for subsetting matrices (two dimensional or 2d) and arrays (larger than two dimensional) is with generalization of one-dimensional (1d) subsetting. This involves with providing a 1d index for each dimension that is separated with a comma. Blank subsetting is useful as well because it allows you to maintain rows or columns.

The following example demonstrates how subsetting works in matrices:

```
> a <- matrix(1:9, nrow = 3)
> colnames(a) <- c("A", "B", "C")
> a[1:2, ]
```

The open bracket "[" simplifies the results with the lowest dimension. Since matrices and arrays are implemented as

150

vectors with special attributes, you can subset them with a single vector. In this case, it will behave as a vector.

In the following example, you will see that arrays are stored in column-major order:

```
> nums <- arr_out(1:4, 1:4, FUN =
"paste", sep = ",")

[,1]  [,2]  [,3]  [,4]

[1] "1,1" "1,2" "1,3" "1,4"

[2] "2,1" "2,2" "2,3" "2,4"  // etc
```

Higher-dimensional data structures can also be subsetted with an integer matrix or a character matrix. In each row, the matrix defines the location with a single value. Each column relates to a dimension within the subsetted array. This means that the 2 column matrix subsets a matrix and the 3 column matrix subsets a 3d array.

The following example shows a vector with values:

```
> vals <- outer(1:5, 1:5, FUN =
"paste", sep = ",")

> select <- matrix(ncol = 2, byrow =
TRUE, c( 1, 1,  3, 1,  2, 4 ))

> vals[select]
```

```
1] "1,1" "3,1" "2,4"
```

## Data Frames

Data frames have the features of lists and matrices. When you subset a single vector, they behave like lists and when you subset two vectors, they behave like matrices.

The following examples show how data frames are used with subsetting:

```
> df <- data.frame(x = 1:3, y = 3:1,
z = letters[1:3])
```

```
>        df[df$x      ==        2,        ]
[1]                   x         y         z
[2] 2 2 2 b
```

```
>                 df[c(1,            3),]
[1]                   x         y         z
[2] 1 1 3 a
```

There are two ways that you can select columns from a data frame. You can do it in a list or a matrix form.

```
// Columns selected in a list form
>              df[c("x",        "z")]
[1]                         x        z
[2] 1 1 a
```

```
// Columns selected like a matrix
>         df[,        c("x",        "z")]
[1]                         x        z
[2] 1 1 a
```

## S3 and S4 Objects

S3 objects consist of atomic vectors, arrays, and lists. They allow you remove an S3 object with the methods that are used in the above examples and applying the concept of the str() function.

The S4 objects include two subsetting operators. They are "**at**" (@) and the "**slot()**" function. The @ is the same as the $ and the slot() is the same as [[. The @ is more constricting than the $ because it returns an error if it detects a slot does not exist.

## Subsetting Operators

The "[[" and "$" subsetting operators are used to simplify and preserve. The "[[" is similar to the "[". The only exception is that it returns a single value and it allows you to remove contents from a list. The dollar operator ($) is the shortened form for the double brackets ([[) combined with the characters for subsetting. Double brackets ([[) are required to work with lists because when the single bracket ([) is applied to a list it will always return a list. The contents of the list are never returned. To get the contents, you will need the double brackets ([[ and the colon (:).

Since it will only return a single value, you need to use the double brackets ([[) with a single positive integer or a string. The following examples will show you how to do this:

```
> a <- list(a = 1, b = 2) a[[1]]
  [1] 1
```

```
>                          a[["a"]]
  [1] 1
```

```
// Vectors are provided to make the
indexes                    recursive.
> b <- list(a = list(b = list(c =
list(d          =          1))))
>    b[[c("a",   "b",   "c",   "d")]]
  [1] 1
```

The above example is same as the following:

```
>          b[["a"]][["b"]][["c"]][["d"]]
[1] 1
```

Since data frames are actually lists of columns, you can use the double brackets ([[) to remove one of the columns from the data frames, for example:

```
> vectnums[[1]], vectnums[["vect1"]]
```

S3 and S4 objects will override the standard behavior of the [ and the [[. They operate in a different way from other object types. The major difference is how you choose how to simplify or preserve the way they behave, as well as determining the default.

Understanding the differences between simplifying and preserving subsetting is essential. Simplifying subsets mean that the simplest form of data structure is returned for the output. It is useful because it provides the result that you are looking for.

Preserving subsetting maintains the structure of the output is the same as the input. It tends to be better for programming because the results will always return the same type. When you omit drop = FALSE when subsetting matrices and data frames you will receive one of the most common programming errors. It will work during testing, but when you pass a single column data frame, you will receive an unexpected error.

When you switch between simplifying and preserving the data types will be different. The following table summarizes the differences between simplifying and preserving for different data types.

| Data Types | Simplifying | Preserving |
|---|---|---|
| Vector | x[[1]] | x[1] |
| List | x[[1]] | x[1] |
| Factor | x[1:4, drop = T] | x[1:4] |
| Array | [1, ] or x[, 1] | x[1, , drop = F] or x[, 1, drop = F] |
| Data frame | x[, 1] or x[[1]] | X[, 1, drop = F] or x[1] |

Data types behave the same way for preserving when inputting and outputting data. Simplifying is slightly different on the other hand. The following examples will explain how the different data types are used:

- **Atomic vector**

```
//The atomic vector removes names.
> x <- c(a = 1, b = 2)
>                                x[1]
[1]                                 a
[2] 1
```

```
x[[1]]
[1] 1
```

- **List**

```
// The object within the list is
returned, but not the elements in a
single                          list.
> y <- list(a = 1, b = 2)
>                         str(y[1])
[1]         List         of        1
[2] $ a: num 1
```

```
>                      str(y[[1]])
[1]   num 1
```

- **Factor**

```
// The factor drops any levels that
are                 not              used.
> z <- factor(c("a", "b"))  z[1]
[1]                  [1]                 a
[2] Levels: a b
```

```
>       z[1,       drop      =      TRUE]
[1] a #> Levels: a
```

- **Matrix** or **Array**

```
// The matrix or array checks for
dimensions that have length 1 and
removes that dimension.

> a <- matrix(1:4, nrow = 2)

> a[1, , drop = FALSE]

[1] [,1] [,2]
```

```
>             3            a[1,              ]
[1] 1 3
```

- **Data frame**

```
// Outputs a single column and
returns a vector instead of a data
frame.
> df <- data.frame(a = 1:2, b = 1:2)
>                          str(df[1])
[1] 'data.frame':    2 obs. of  1
variable:
[2]  $ a: int  1 2
```

```
>                        str(df[[1]])
[1]  int [1:2] 1 2
```

```
> str(df[, "a", drop = FALSE])
[1] 'data.frame':    2 obs. of  1
variable:
[2] $ a: int  1 2
```

```
> str(df[, "a"])
[1]  int [1:2] 1 2
```

The dollar operator ($) is a short form operator, for example x$y is the same as x[["y", exact = FALSE]]. It is widely used to access variables within a data frame.

It is a mistake to use the dollar operator ($) when you have the name of a column stored in a variable. In the following examples you will see how it is incorrectly used and what to use instead.

```
>            var         <-          "cyl"
// Doesn't  work    -   mycars$var
translated  to   mycars[["var"]]
mycars$var
[1] NULL
```

```
// Instead  use  [[  mycars[[var]]
[1] 6 6 4 6 8 6 8 4 4 6 6 8 8 8 8 8
8 4 4 4 4 8 8 8 8 4 4 4 8 6 8 4
```

One major difference between $ and [[. The $ operator performs partial matching, as you will see in the following example:

```
>  x  <-  list(abc  =  1)  x$a
[1]         1       x[["a"]]
[2]NULL
```

To prevent this from happening, you will need to set the global option "**warnPartialMatchDollar**" to TRUE. You should carefully use it because it may affect the behavior in other codes, such as packages.

Sometime you experience some unusual behavior because of missing or out of bounds (OOB) indices. When you use the single bracket ([) and double brackets ([[), for example, you may notice some unusual behavior when the index is out of bounds. This may happen because you may try to remove a four-length vector or subset a vector with NA or NULL. The following examples show how these operators are used in this manner:

```
// Removing a four length vector
> x <- 1:4 str(x[5])

//Subset a vector with NA
> int NA str(x[NA_real_])
```

```
// Subset a vector with NULL
> int NA str(x[NULL]) #> int(0)
```

The following table provides a summary of results for subsetting atomic vectors and lists using the [ and [[, as well as other out of bounds (OOB) values.

| Operator | Index | Atomic | List |
|---|---|---|---|
| [ | OOB | NA | list(NULL) |
| [ | NA_real | NA | list(NULL) |
| [ | NULL | x[0] | list(NULL) |

| [[ | OOB | Error | Error |
|----|---------|-------|-------|
| [[ | NA_real | Error | NULL |
| [[ | NULL | Error | Error |

When the vector is named, the names of OOB, missing, or NULL will be "<NA>".

## Subset Assignments

R allows you to establish sub assignments, combine subsetting and assignments so you can modify different parts of objects. You can combine subsetting operators when making assignments. They are used to modify selected values for the input vector.

The following examples shows when you can and cannot apply subset assignments:

```
>          x           <-          1:5
>    x[c(1,   2)]     <-    2:3    x
[1] 2 3 3 4 5
```

```
// Match the length of Left Hand
Side (LHS) with the Right Hand
Side (RHS)
>        x[-1]        <-        4:1        x
[1] 2 4 3 2 1
```

162

```
// Does not checking for duplicate
indices.
>     x[c(1,    1)]    <-    2:3    x
[1] 3 4 3 2 1
```

```
// Integers cannot be combined with
NA  -  You  will  receive  an  error.
>    x[c(1,    NA)]    <-    c(1,    2)
Error in x[c(1, NA)] <- c(1, 2): NAs
are    not    allowed    in    subscripted
assignments.

// A valid combination of logical
indices    with    NA    -    treated    as
"false".
>    x[c(T,    F,    NA)]    <-    1    x
[1] 1 4 3 1 1
```

```
// This  is  for  modifying  vectors
conditionally.
> vt <- data.frame(a = c(1, 10, NA))
>    vt$a[vt$a    <    5]    <-    0    vt$a
[1]  0 10 NA
```

You can subset with nothing along with assignments it
helps to keep the original object class and structure.
Evaluate the following two statements to get a better
understanding.

163

```
// The "mycars" object remains as a
data                               frame.
>    mtcars[]    <-    lapply(mtcars,
as.integer)
```

```
// The "mycars" object becomes a
list.
>    mtcars    <-    lapply(mtcars,
as.integer)
```

Lists allow you to use subsetting with assignments and NULL, to remove specific contents in a list. If you would like to insert a literal NULL, use the [ and list(NULL). The following examples show how to use NULL with lists:

```
>  x  <-  list(a  =  1,  b  =  2)
> x[["b"]] <- NULL str(x)
```

```
//      Show      a      list      of      1
>        $        a:        num        1
>     y    <-    list(a    =    1)
> y["b"] <- list(NULL) str(y)
```

```
//      Shows      a      list      of      2
>        $        a:        num        1
>  $ b: NULL
```

Assignments to subsets have a special structure that have may look like the following complex assignment:

164

```
> x[2:4] <- 10:12
```

The result of the above statement after it has been executed, actually appears like the following statements:

```
>          '*tmp*'              <-          x
>    x    <-    "[<-"('*tmp*',    2:4,
value=10:12)
> rm('*tmp*')
```

In the above example, the index is converted first to a numeric index and then the elements are replaced in a sequential format with numeric index. It behaves like a for loop. Any variable with the name "*tmp* will be overridden and removed, therefore this variable name should not used within the code.

The same concept can be applied to functions, other than using the open bracket ([). The function that is being replaced will have the same name. The last argument in the code must be a new value that will be assigned. In the following example, you will see how this is done:

```
> names(x) <- c("a","b")
```

This example is also the same as the following statements:

```
>              `*tmp*`              <-              x
>      x       <-       "names<-"(`*tmp*`,
value=c("a","b"))
> rm(`*tmp*`)
```

Additionally, when you nest complex statement, it should be evaluated recursively, like in the following example:

```
> names(x)[3] <- "Three"
```

This example is the same as the following statements:

```
> `*tmp*` <- x
> x <- "names<-"(`*tmp*`, value="[<-
"(names(`*tmp*`), 3, value="Three"))
> rm(`*tmp*`)
```

Complex assignments also allows you to the use the <<- operators within the enclosing environment. Here is an example of how it is used:

```
> names(x)[3] <<- "Three".
```

This example is also same as the following statements:

```
>            '*tmp*'        <<-         get(x,
envir=parent.env(),    inherits=TRUE)
>    names('*tmp*')[3]    <-    "Three"
>        x          <<-         '*tmp*'
> rm('*tmp*')
```

```
>              '*tmp*'                  <-
get(x,envir=parent.env(),
inherits=TRUE)
>    x      <<-      "names<-"('*tmp*',
value="[<-"(names('*tmp*'),          3,
value="Three"))
> rm('*tmp*')
```

In the above example, only the target variable is evaluated within the enclosing environment. The following example will show you how it works:

```
>                         e<-c(a=1,b=2)
> i<-1
```

```
>                            local({
>        e        <-      c(A=10,B=11)
>                  i                <-2
> e[i] <<- e[i]+1})
```

In this example, the local value of "I" is used on the LHS

167

and RHS. The same is true for the local value "e" on the RHS of the super assignment statement. The value "e" is set outside to "**ab**". The super assignment is actually the same as the following statements:

```
>         `*tmp*`         <-        get(e,
envir=parent.env(),      inherits=TRUE)
>         `*tmp*`[i]      <-        e[i]+1
>         e              <<-        `*tmp*`
> rm(`*tmp*`)
```

This example is the same as the following:

```
x[is.na(x)] <<- 0
```

This is also the same as these statements:

```
>         `*tmp*`                  <-
get(x,envir=parent.env(),
inherits=TRUE)
>         `*tmp*`[is.na(x)]        <-        0
>         x              <<-        `*tmp*`
> rm(`*tmp*`)
```

However, it is not the same as the following statements:

```
>         `*tmp*`                  <-
get(x,envir=parent.env(),
inherits=TRUE)
>     `*tmp*`[is.na(`*tmp*`)]      <-        0
>         x              <<-        `*tmp*`
> rm(`*tmp*`)
```

The two above observations are different if there is the local variable "x". It is recommended that you should avoid using a local variable with the same name as the target variable of any super assignment. This code should only be used when it is absolutely necessary.

## Applying Subsetting

Subsetting is often applied to solve problems in data analysis, but you can use it in several other applications. In the above examples, you learned about some basic concepts that you could use to build efficient applications. In this section, you will learn more about applying those basic techniques with functions, such as subset, merge, and plyr::arrange(). You will understand how they are implemented in subsetting, so you can create flexible applications.

The following applications will help you properly implement subsetting so you can create flexible applications.

**Application 1: Use Character Matching to Create Lookup Tables.**

Character matching allows you to create lookup table. If you would like to convert abbreviations for instance, you would to do the following:

```
// Creating and defining
abbreviations
x <- c("m", "f", "u", "f", "f", "m",
"m")
lookup <- c(m = "Male", f =
"Female", u = NA)
lookup[x]
```

```
// The results for the abbreviations
>         m       f        u
f         f        m        m  #
>    "Male" "Female"        NA
"Female" "Female"  "Male"  "Male"
```

```
// Characters are undefined. Use the
unname() function to remove the
names    from    the    results.
unname(lookup[x])
[1]   "Male"        "Female"  NA
"Female" "Female" "Male"   "Male"
```

```
// Fewer output results are
specified and returned
c(m = "Known", f = "Known", u =
"Unknown")[x]
>  m          f          u          f

f            m                     m
>  "Known"       "Known"    "Unknown"
"Known"    "Known"    "Known"    "Known"
```

## Application 2: Matching and Merging: Integer Subsetting

Sometimes you may have a complicated lookup table with multiple columns of information. If you have a vector integer and a table with property description, you could use the following expressions, for example:

```
> grades <- c(1, 2, 2, 3, 1)
> info <- data.frame( grade = 3:1,
> desc = c("Excellent", "Good",
"Poor"), fail = c(F, F, T) )
```

If you want to duplicate the "**info**" table in the above example to have a row for each value in the "**grades**" object, you do so in two ways. You can either use the "**match()**" function and integer subsetting or you can use the "**rownames()**" function and character subsetting. The following examples show the two ways:

```
// The contents of the "grades"
object are returned.
> grades
[1] 1 2 2 3 1

// The match() function is
implemented.
> id <- match(grades, info$grade)
> info[id, ]
```

```
// The match() function returns the
following results in a table form.
>                grade   desc   fail
> 3               1             Poor    TRUE
> 2               2             Good  FALSE //
etc...
```

```
// The rownames() function is
implemented.
> rownames(info) <- info$grade
> info[as.character(grades), ]
```

```
// The rownames() function returns
the following results in a table
form.
>           grade            desc   fail
> 1             1            Poor   TRUE
> 2             2            Good  FALSE //
etc...
```

If you would like to match multiple columns, you will first need to shrink them into a single column. This means that you will need to use the interaction(), paste() or plyr::id() functions. You can also use the merge() or plyr::join() functions to accomplish the same results. You will need to review the source code to accomplish this technique.


**Application 3: Random Samples/Bootstrap: Integer Subsetting**

You can use integer indices to perform random sampling or bootstrapping of a vector or a data frame. The sample() function can be used to generate a vector of indices and then use subsetting to access the value. The following example will help understand this concept:

```
// Object is implemented for the
data                         frame
> df <- data.frame(x = rep(1:3, each
= 2), y = 6:1, z = letters[1:6])
```

```
// The seeds are set to reproduce
set.seed(10)
```

```
// Object defines a random order
> df[sample(nrow(df)), ]
```

```
// Values are returned in a random
order.
>                    x      y      z
>          4         2      3      d
> 2 1 5 b // etc...
```

```
// Three random rows are selected.
> df[sample(nrow(df), 3), ]
```

```
// The results for three random
rows.
>                    x      y      z
>          2         1      5      b
>          6         3      1      f
> 3 2 4 c
```

```
// Six  bootstrap  replicates  are
selected.
> df[sample(nrow(df), 6, rep = T), ]
// Six  results  are  returned.
        x           y           z
>       3           2     4      c
> 4     2 3 d //etc
```

The arguments within the sample() function controls the number of samples to be extracted. They also determine whether the sampling can be done with or without a replacement.

## Application 4: Ordering: Integer Subsetting

The order() function is used to take a vector as input and return it as an integer vector. It describes how the subsetted vector should be ordered.

In the following example, you will see how the order() function is implemented to order subsetted vectors:

```
//Order() takes a vector as a input
>   x    <-    c("b",    "c",    "a")
>                        order(x)
[1] 3 1 2
```

176

```
// A vector is returned as an
integer                        vector
>                        x[order(x)]
> [1] "a" "b" "c"
```

To sever the relationship, you can provide additional variables to the order() function and change it from ascending to descending order by using "**decreasing = TRUE**". Any missing values will be placed at the end of the vector by default, however you can remove the missing values with "**na.last = NA**" insert it at the front with "**na.last = FALSE**".

If you have two or more dimensions, use the order() function and integer subsetting to make it easier to order the rows or the columns of an object. The following examples show how to order the rows and columns of an object.

```
// Implementation of a randomly
reordered                        row.
> df2 <- df[sample(nrow(df)), 3:1]
```

```
//      Randomly    reordered    row.
df2
>                 z         y         x
>        3        c         4         2
> 1 a 6 1 // etc...
```

```
//       An       ordered       row
>        df2[order(df2$x),            ]
>                 z         y         x
>        1        a         6         1
> 2 b 5 1 // etc
```

```
// An ordered row with character
names.
df2[,            order(names(df2))]
>                 x         y         z
>        3        2         4         c
> 1 1 6 a // etc
```

There are also other functions that are available for sorting vectors, such as sort(), data frames, and plyr::arrange().`

## Application 5: Expanded Group Counts: Integer Subsetting

You may get a data frame with identical collapsed rows with an added count column. To open the data, you would use the rep() function by subsetting it with a recurrent row.

In the following example, the rep() function is used to accomplish this task.

```
> df <- data.frame(x = c(2, 4, 1), y
= c(9, 11, 6), n = c(3, 5, 1))
>        rep(1:nrow(df),          df$n)
> [1] 1 1 1 2 2 2 2 2 3
```

```
df[rep(1:nrow(df),        df$n),         ]
>                    x         y         n
>        1           2         9         3
> 1.1 2   9 3 // etc...
```

## Application 6: Remove Column from Data Frames: Character Subsetting

There are methods for removing columns from a data from. You can set individual columns to NULL or you can subset so you can only return the columns you want.

The following examples show how to set the columns to NULL and return specific columns:

```
// Columns are set to NULL
> df <- data.frame(x = 1:3, y = 3:1,
z             =             letters[1:3])
> df$z <- NULL
```

```
// Specific  columns  are  returned.
> df <- data.frame(x = 1:3, y = 3:1,
z = letters[1:3])
```

```
df[c("x",                          "y")]
>                        x           y
>          1            1           3
>          2            2           2
> 3 3 1
```

If you already know columns that you do not want, you can set the operations to only keep the columns that you want. Here is how you could do it:

```
df[setdiff(names(df),              "z")]
>                        x           y
>          1            1           3
> 2 2 2 3 3 1
```

## Application 7: Select Rows based on Condition: Logical Subsetting

Logical subsetting allows you to conveniently combine conditions from multiple columns. It is possibly one of the most widely used method for removing rows from a data frame. The following example shows how to properly select rows using logical subsetting.

180

```
mycars[mycars$gear    ==    5,    ]
> mpg cyl   disp   hp drat wt   qsec
vs              am      gear      carb
> 27 26.0    4 120.3   91 4.43 2.140
16.7    0    1         5          2
> 28 30.4    4  95.1 113 3.77 1.513
16.9  1  1    5     2 // etc...
```

```
mtcars[mtcars$gear == 5 & mtcars$cyl
==           4,              ]
> mpg cyl   disp   hp drat     wt qsec
vs         am         gear      carb
> 27 26.0    4 120.3   91 4.43 2.140
16.7    0    1         5          2
> 28 30.4    4  95.1 113 3.77 1.513
16.9  1  1    5     2
```

**Note:** Remember to use the vector Boolean operators "&" and "|" instead of the "&&" and "||" operators. Use DeMorgan's laws to simplify negations.

**Important:**

!(X & Y) is the same as !X | !Y

!(X | Y) is the same as !X & !Y

In a nutshell, !(X & !(Y | Z)) simplifies to !X | !!(Y|Z) and then to !X | Y | Z.

The subset() function is a shortened function for subsetting data frames. It saves time on typing, because it minimizes repeating the data frame name.

The following examples shows how to implement the subset() function:

```
> subset(mycars, gear == 5)
> mpg cyl  disp  hp drat    wt qsec
vs       am        gear      carb
> 27 26.0   4 120.3   91 4.43 2.140
16.7     0   1          5         2
> 28 30.4   4  95.1 113 3.77 1.513
16.9  1  1   5     2 // etc...
```

```
subset(mycars, gear == 5 & cyl == 4)
> mpg cyl  disp  hp drat    wt qsec
vs       am        gear      carb
> 27 26.0   4 120.3   91 4.43 2.140
16.7     0   1          5         2
> 28 30.4   4  95.1 113 3.77 1.513
16.9  1  1   5     2
```

## Application 8: Boolean Algebra VS Sets: Logical & Integer Subsetting

It is important to know the equivalence between set operations (integer subsetting) and Boolean algebra(logical

182

subsetting). It is more effective to use set operations in the following situations:

- To find the first or last TRUE statements.

- When using only a few TRUE statement and many FALSE statements. Using set expressions is faster and require less storage.

The "**which()**" function allows you to convert a Boolean expression to an integer expression. There is no reverse operation in R, but you can create one. The following example shows how you can do this:

```
>    x    <-    sample(10)    <    4
>                              which(x)
 [1]   3   7 10
```

```
unwhich    <-    function(x,    n)
{        out    <-    rep_len(FALSE,    n)
out[x] <- TRUE    out }
```

```
unwhich(which(x),                  10)
 [1]  FALSE FALSE   TRUE FALSE FALSE
FALSE  TRUE FALSE FALSE   TRUE
```

The following example will show you how to create two logical vectors and integers that are equivalent. After

183

learning this concept, you will see the relationship between Boolean and set operations.

```
> (x1 <- 1:10 %% 2 == 0)
 [1] FALSE  TRUE FALSE  TRUE FALSE
TRUE FALSE  TRUE FALSE  TRUE
```

```
> (x2 <- which(x1))
 [1]     2     4     6     8    10
> (y1 <- 1:10 %% 5 == 0)
 [1] FALSE FALSE FALSE FALSE  TRUE
FALSE FALSE FALSE FALSE  TRUE
(y2                    which(y1))
> [1]  5 10
```

```
// X & Y <-> intersect(x, y)
x1              &              y1
 [1] FALSE FALSE FALSE FALSE FALSE
FALSE FALSE FALSE FALSE  TRUE
```

```
>           intersect(x2,        y2)
 [1] 10
```

```
// X | Y <-> union(x, y)
>           x1           |           y1
 [1] FALSE  TRUE FALSE  TRUE  TRUE
TRUE FALSE  TRUE FALSE  TRUE
```

```
>                union(x2,               y2)
 [1]   2   4   6   8  10   5
```

```
//   X   &   !Y   <->   setdiff(x,   y)
>             x1              &           !y1
[1] FALSE    TRUE FALSE    TRUE FALSE
TRUE FALSE    TRUE FALSE FALSE
```

```
setdiff(x2,                           y2)
[1] 2 4 6 8
```

```
> xor(X, Y) < - > setdiff(union(x,
y), intersect(x, y))
>              xor(x1,              y1)
[1] FALSE    TRUE FALSE    TRUE    TRUE
TRUE FALSE    TRUE FALSE FALSE
```

```
>        setdiff(union(x2,          y2),
intersect(x2,                       y2))
[1] 2 4 6 8 5
```

Initially, when you start learning subsetting you may incorrectly use "**x[which(y)]**" instead of "**x[y]**". Under these circumstances, which() will provide any results. Instead it changes from logical to integer subsetting and produce the exact same result. You should also be aware that the "**x[which(y)]**" is not the same as "**x[!y]:**". If **y** is all FALSE, "**which(y)**" will be "**integer(0)**" and "-integer(0)" will still be "**integer(0)**". Therefore, you will not receive any values. In a nutshell, you should avoid changing from logical to integer subsetting you want the first or last TRUE value, for example.

# Vectors

Vectors are considered adjoining cells that contains data. You can access the cells by indexing specific operations, such as x[5]. R provides six basic atomic vectors. They are logical, integer, real, complex, raw, and string/character. Modes and storage modes for the different vector types are specified in the following table:

| Typeof | Mode | Storage Mode |
|---|---|---|
| Logical | Logical | Logical |
| Lnteger | Numeric | Integer |
| Double | Numeric | Double |
| Complex | Complex | Complex |
| Character | Character | Character |
| Raw | Raw | Raw |

Some examples of vectors include single numbers, such as 3.5, and strings, such as "two single vectors". Generally, vectors have a length 1, but vectors with length 0 are also considered useful. String vectors have a "character" mode and storage mode. Single elements of characters are considered character strings.

A vector can also be considered as a sequence that contains data elements with the same data type. The elements within the vector are officially called components. There are many different types of vectors and different ways that you can apply them.

The following examples show different ways you input vectors into R.

**Example 1:** Vector with Numeric Values

```
// Vector   contains   three   numeric
values,       3,       5,       and       7.
> c(3, 5, 7)
[1] 2 3 5
```

**Example 2:** Vector with Logical Values

```
//Vector   contains   logical   values.
> c(TRUE, FALSE, TRUE, FALSE, FALSE)

[1]   TRUE FALSE   TRUE FALSE FALSE
```

**Example 3:** Vector with Character Strings

```
//    Vector    contains    character
strings.
> c("aa", "bb", "cc", "dd", "ee")
[1] "aa" "bb" "cc" "dd" "ee"
```

**Example 4:** Vector Returns Length

```
Elements  in  a  vector  using  the
length() function. The length of the
function         is         returned.
> length(c("aa", "bb", "cc", "dd", "
ee"))
[1] 5
```

Vectors are manipulated in many different ways. The following examples will show you different ways to manipulate vectors.

- **Combining Vectors:** Vectors maybe combined with the c() function. The following two vectors "a" and "b" are combined to create a new vector that contains elements from the two vectors.

```
> a = c(3, 5, 7)
> b = c("aa", "bb", "cc", "dd", "ee"
)
> c(a, b)
[1] "3"  "5"  "7"  "aa" "bb" "cc" "d
d" "ee"
```

In the above example, you will see that the numeric values are forced into character strings when the two vectors are combined. This is necessary because it maintains the old data type for the elements within the same vector.

- **Vector Arithmetic**: Vector arithmetic operations are performed element by element, for example:

```
> a = c(1, 3, 5, 7)
> b = c(2, 4, 6, 8)
```

If you multiply "a" by 5, you would get a vector that multiplied each element by 2.

```
> 2 * a
[1] 2 6 10 14
```

If you add vector "**a**" by vector "**b**", the sum would result in a vector where the elements are the sum of the corresponding elements of a and b.

```
> a + b
[1]  3  7  11 15
```

You can also subtract, multiply, and divide corresponding vectors. When you perform the respective operations with the elements, you will get new vectors.

**Example 1:** Subtract Vectors

```
a - b
[1]  -1  -1  -1 -1
```

## Example 2: Multiply Vectors

```
> a * b
[1]  2  12  35 56
```

## Example 3: Divide Vectors

```
> a / b
[1] 0.5 0.75 0.83 0.875
```

- **Recycling Rule:** In vector arithmetic, there is a recycling rule, where two vectors have unequal length. The shorter one is recycled to match the longer vector. In the following example, vectors "**a**" and "**b**" have different lengths and calculate totals by recycling the values of the shorter vector "**b**".

```
> a = c(5, 10, 15)
> b = c(1, 2, 3, )
> a + b
[1] 6, 12, 18
```

- **Vector Index:** Vectors are retrieved by declaring an index within a square bracket ([ ]) operator. In the following example, you will see how to retrieve a vector element. Since the vector index is 1, the 3rd index position is used to retrieve the third element.

```
> a = c("vv",        "ww", "xx", "yy",
"zz")
> a[3]
[1] "xx"
```

The square bracket operator returns more results than other programming languages. The results of the square bracket is actually different vector, and produce the vector s[3] with a single element "**cc**".

- **Negative Index:** If you have a negative index, it would remove the element that has a position with the same absolute value and the negative index. In the following example a vector is generated when the third element is removed.

```
> s[-3]
[1] "vv" "ww" "yy" "zz"
```

- **Out of Range Indexes:** When an index is out of range, a missing value is reported through the "**NA**" symbol, as seen in the following example:

```
>s[10]
[1] NA
```

- **Numeric Index Vector:** New vectors can be sliced from a specific vector with a numeric index vector that consists of elements for the original to be retrieved. In the following example you will see how to retrieve a vector slice that contains the fourth and fifth element of a given vector "**a**".

```
> a = c("vv", "ww", "xx", "yy", "zz"
)
> a[c(4, 5)]
[1] "yy" "zz"
```

- **Duplicate Indexes:** Index vectors allow you to duplicate values. The In the following example, an element is retrieved two times in a single operation.

```
> s[c(1,                           3)]
[1] "vv" "xx" "xx"
```

- **Out of Order Index Vectors:** Index vectors can also be generated out of order. In the following example, a vector slice produces first and second elements that are reversed.

```
> s[c(2, 1, 3)]
[1] "ww" "vv" "xx"
```

- **Range Index:** A vector slice can created between two indexes by using the colon ":" operator. This works well for situations that involve large vectors.

```
> s[2:5]
[1] "ww" "xx" "yy" "zz"
```

- **Logical Index Vector:** New vectors can be sliced and a vector is given with a logical index vector that has the same length as the original vector. The elements are TRUE for the corresponding elements in the original vector that is included in the vector slice, and it is FALSE if it is not.

Review the following example with the vector "**a**" of length "**5**" for a better understanding:

```
> a = c("vv", "ww", "xx", "yy", "zz"
)
```

If you would like to retrieve the second and fifth elements of "a", you could create a logical vector L with the same length and have the second and fifth elements set to TRUE.

```
> L = c(FALSE, TRUE, FALSE, FALSE, TRUE)
> a[L]
[1] "ww" "zz"
```

- **Named Vector Elements:** Vector elements can have assigned names. In the following example, the following variable "**n**" is a character string vector that contains three elements.

```
> n = c("Mary", "Ann",    "Jane")
> n
[1] "Mary" "Ann" "Jane"
```

If you name the first element as "First", the second as "Middle", and the third element as "Last", you would use the statements to generate the following example:

```
> names(n) = c("First", "Middle", "Last")
> n
 [1]    First    Middle    Last
 [2] "Mary" "Sue"  "Jane"
```

You could also retrieve the Last element by using its name.

195

```
>                              n["Last"]
> [1] "Jane"
```

Additionally, you can reverse the order with the character string index vector.

```
> v[c("First", "Middle",    "Last")]
>                       Middle First
[1] "Sue" "Jane"
```

You will learn more about different ways to implement vectors later on in this chapter.

## Vectors and Assignments

R uses named data structures to manipulate vectors. The simplest structure is the numeric. It is a single entity that consists of a structured collection of numbers. If you would like to set a vector "x" with five number, for example, 3.3, 4.4. 5.2, 6.7, and 30.4, you would use the following statement:

```
> x <- c(3.3, 4.4, 5.2, 6.7, 30.4)
```

The above assignment statement uses the c() function. In this context, can take a random number of vector arguments with a vector value obtained from concatenation of end-to-end arguments. A number that occurs independently in a statement is taken as a vector with length 1.

If you notice the assignment operator (<-) consists of two characters, as was mentioned earlier. This is repeated to establish the connection between vectors and assignments. The less than (<) and minus (-) characters are used beside each other to create the assignment operator. They point to the object that receives the value of the statement. In many situations, the equal (=) operator is used as an alternative. You can also use the assign() function to establish an assignment.

The following example shows how the assign() function is used to assign vectors:

```
> assign("x", c((3.3, 4.4, 5.2, 6.7,
30.4))
```

The typical assignment operator (<-) used in the above example, is considered the short form. As mentioned earlier, you can use this operator in the opposite direction to assign vectors, for example:

```
> c((3.3, 4.4, 5.2, 6.7, 30.4))-> x
```

# Vector Types

Vectors are considered the most important object in R, but they are others that are formally used.

Here is a list of some formal objects that are used in R:

1. **Matrices:** Matrices or arrays are multi-dimensional generalizations of vectors. They are vectors that maybe used to index two or more indices that can be outputted in different ways.

2. **Factors:** Factors provide solid ways for handling data from different categories.

3. **Lists:** Lists haven a general vector form, where various elements do not have to have the same type. These are often vectors or lists. Lists are conveniently used to return the results of some statistical calculations.

4. **Data Frames:** Data frames are matrices that are similar to structures, where the columns can have different data types. You can look at data frames as "data matrices", where one row is possibly an observational unit with both numerical and categorical variables. Data frames are categorical, but the responses are numerical.

5. **Functions:** Functions are considered objects in R that are stored in the project's workspace.

## Character Vectors

Character quantities and character vectors are widely used in R. They are used for plot labels, for examples. When necessary they are indicated by a sequence of characters that are delimited by the double quote character ("), for example, "x-vectors" and "New iteration values".

Character strings are used either with the double quotes (") or single quotes('), but are outputted with the double quotes or without any quotes. The C type back slash (\) escape characters are used, therefore the double back slash (\\) is entered and outputted as \\, and the inside double quotes (") are entered as a single back slash (\). Other helpful escape sequences, such \n, newline, \b, tab, \t, and backspace are also used. You can also use character vectors to concatenate a vector using the c() function.

The paste() function is used to take random arguments and concatenate them individually into character strings. Arguments that are numbers are forced into character strings the same way they are printed. The arguments separated by default within the results by a single blank character. This can be altered by using "**sep=string**". This argument uses changes the character to a possible empty string.

The following example will show you how the paste() function is used to convert into character vectors:

```
// The "labs" variable is changed
into    the    character    vector.
> labs <- paste(c("A","B"), 1:10,
sep="")
> c("A1", "B2", "A3", "B4", "A5",
"B6", "A7", "B8", "A9", "B10")
```

Notice in the above example that short lists are recycled, therefore c("A", "B") is repeated five time to match the sequence 1:10.

## Logical Vectors

R allows the manipulation of logical vectors. The elements of logical vectors may have TRUE, FALSE, and Not Available (NA) values. The TRUE and FALSE values are often abbreviated to T and F respectively. They are short form variables that are set to TRUE and FALSE, by default. They are not reserved words and therefore can be overwritten by the user. Therefore, it is better to write the full words, TRUE and FALSE.

Logical vectors are created by conditions, as you shown in the following example:

```
> temp <- x > 13
```

The above statement sets the **"temp"** variable as a vector with same length as **"x"** with FALSE values that correspond to the elements of x. This is where the condition is FALSE. The logical operators (<, <=, >, >=, ==) are used for equality and the != operator for not equal. Additionally, if v1 and v2 are logical expressions, then (!) operator is used.

Logical vectors can be used in ordinary arithmetic, where they are forced as numeric vectors and FALSE becomes 0 and TRUE becomes 1. There are certain logical vectors that have related numbers that are not equal.

Typically, the first step to establishing a vector is to define a vector with data, and the second step is to define a vector with logical values. When logical values are used for the index into the vector of data values, only the elements that correspond to the variables that are set to TRUE are returned. The following example will show you how it works:

```
>        x          <-        c(1,2,3,4,5)
>                 y                      <-
c(TRUE,FALSE,FALSE,TRUE,FALSE)
> x[y] [1] 1 4
```

```
>         max(x[y])          [1]          4
> sum(x[y]) [1] 5
```

Logical vectors are actual part of a logical expression and any logical expression can be used an index that opens many possibilities. For instance, you can remove or focus on elements that match specific requirements. In the following example, you see how to remove all the elements over a specific value:

```
>        x        =        c(6,2,5,3,8,2)
>    x   [1]   6   2   5   3   8   2
>              y          =          x[x>5]
> y [1] 6 8
```

In another example, if you would like to join values that match two different factors in another vector, you could write the following statements:

```
> x =
data.frame(one=as.factor(c('a','a','
b','b','c','c')),
two=c(1,2,3,4,5,6))
> x    one two 1   a    1 2    a    2 3
b    3 4    b    4 5    c    5 6    c    6
> values   =   x$two[(x$one=='a')   |
(x$one=='a')]
> values [1] 1 2 3 4
```

In the above example, the single or (|) operator is used. This operator has a different meaning from the double or (||) operators. The single or (|) operator performs a vector operator on a term-by-term basis, whereas the double (||) or operators evaluates and statement and produce and TRUE or FALSE result. The following example will show you how this is done:

```
> (c(TRUE,TRUE))|(c(FALSE,TRUE))  [1]
TRUE  TRUE

>     (c(TRUE,TRUE))||(c(FALSE,TRUE))
[1] TRUE

> (c(TRUE,TRUE))&(c(FALSE,TRUE))  [1]
FALSE    TRUE

>     (c(TRUE,TRUE))&&(c(FALSE,TRUE))
[1] FALSE
```

## Not Available(NA) Values

Data entries that are marked NA can be a problem. The predefined variable NA is used to indicate that there is missing information. The problem in this case is that some of the functions will return an error if one of elements in the data is NA. There are some functions that will allow you to ignore these missing values, like the one shown in the following example:

```
>      x         <-        c(1,2,3,4,NA)
> x [1]    1    2    3    4    NA
>         sum(x)          [1]        NA
> sum(x,na.rm=TRUE) [1] 10
```

On the other hand, there are times when this solution is not available or you may just want to omit the NA values. In this case, you can use the is.na() function to determine which items that are not available. The not (!) operator is used for indexing the items within a vector that has NA values. The following example shows how the is.na() function is used to accomplish this.

```
>        x          <-          c(1,2,3,4,NA)
> is.na(x)  [1]  FALSE   FALSE   FALSE
FALSE                                    TRUE
> !is.na(x)  [1]   TRUE    TRUE    TRUE
TRUE FALSE
```

```
>   x[!is.na(x)]   [1]   1   2   3   4
>        y         <-        x[!is.na(x)]
> y [1] 1 2 3 4
```

## Generic Vectors

Generic vectors or Lists are used to for storing data elements. Each element may contain any type of R object. This means that the elements do not have to have the same data type. You can be access list elements by using three different indexing operations. They are lists, matrices, and multi-dimensional arrays.

The basic vector types are considered atomic vectors when lists are excluded. Another list form is pairlists. They are handled the same way as generic vectors. Elements within pairlists for instance are accessed using the [ [ ] ] syntax. Using pairlists are not as widely used, because it is believed that generic vectors are more efficient. When you access an internal pairlist in R, it is typically converted to a generic vector.

## Numeric Vectors

Numeric vectors are used to create or force objects with the "numeric" type. In general, the "is.numeric" and "as.numeric" are used to test objects to be interpreted as numbers. The following syntaxes are used to implement the applicable numeric() functions:

```
>       numeric(length      =        0)
>          as.numeric(x,            ...)
> is.numeric(x)
```

The following details will help you better understand the arguments used in the numeric(), as.numeric(), and is.numeric() functions:

- **length:** The "length" argument is a positive or non-negative integer that specifies the required length. Double values are converted to integers, which provides a length argument.
- **x:** The "x" argument is used to represent an object that will be used or tested.
- ... : The periods (...) are additional arguments that are passed to and from methods that are used elsewhere

Here is some additional information about each of the numeric functions.

- **Numeric()** : The numeric() function are similar to the double or real data type, where they create a double-precision vector with a specific length for each element that is equal to 0.

- **as.numeric()**: The as.numeric() function is a generic function, but you must use S3 (objects, generic functions, and methods) methods written for the as.double() function because it is the same as the as.double.

- **is.numeric()**: The is.numeric() function is an internal generic primitive function that can be used to write methods that handle specific classes for objects. It is not the same as the is.double() function. The factors are managed by the default method. The methods used for the is.numeric() function should only return TRUE if the base type is double, integer, or if the values are numeric. The default method returns TRUE if the argument has the "numeric" type (i.e. double or integer) associated to it and not a factor. Otherwise, it is FALSE. This means that you would use one of the following syntax to implement the vector:

```
is.integer(x)      ||    is.double(x),    or
(mode(x) == "numeric") && !is.factor(x)
```

The as.numeric() and is.numeric() functions are S4 generic, therefore you set methods for them by using setMethod. To have as.numeric and as.double stay identical, you can only set S4 methods for as.numeric. S4 classes or methods are stricter than S3 and uses the following syntax:

```
setClass([class                name],
representation  =  [field  names],
[prototype     object] contains   =
[superclass])
```

R uses the double and numeric floating point vectors, where "double" and "numeric" data types are used to define values. The numeric type is name of the mode, as well as the implicit class. For an S4 formal class you would use "numeric". It calt can be confusing because the mode "numeric" also means "double" or "integer" and may conflict with S4 classes or methods. Actually, "is.numeric" tests the mode and not the class, but "as.numeric" (identical to "as.double") is directed towards the class.

## Index Vectors

Vector with subsets can be selected by changing to the vector name of the index vector that is within the square brackets. Generally, any expressions that evaluates to a vector can have subsets in the same way as changing the index within the square bracket after the statement.

These index vectors may have any of the following four distinct types:

1. **Logical Vector:** A logical vector used with an index vector is reused with the same length as the vectors selected from the elements that will be selected. The values that are TRUE in the index vector are chosen and the ones that are FALSE are deleted. For example, if y <- x[!is.na(x)] creates (or re-creates) an object y that contains a value x that is not lost or have the same order. If x has missing values, then y is going to be shorter than x.

```
>(x+1) [(!is.na(x)) & x>0] -> z
```

210

The above statement creates an object z that will replace the values of the vector "x+1", that has the corresponding value in x, that is not missing and positive.

2. **Positive Integral Vector:** When a vector has positive integers, the values within the index vector must be in the set "**{1, 2, , .., length(X)}**". The elements that correspond to the vector are selected and then concatenated within the result. The index vector can have any length. Likewise, the result has the same length as the index vector. For example, "**x[5]**" would be the fifth element of x and "**>[1:15]**" would select the first fifteen (15) elements of x – assuming the length(x) is not less than 15.

```
>          c("a","b") [rep(c(1,2,2,1),
times=4)]
```

The above statement produces a character of length 16 that consists of "a", "b", "b", "a" that is repeated four times.

3. **Negative Integral Vector:** When a vector has negative integers, the index vector specifies the values that will be omitted only. The following example shows the implementation of a negative

integral vector.

```
// The first five elements of x are
not                       implemented.
> y <- x[-(1:5)]
```

4. **Character Vector:** A vector of character strings is only possible when an object with the names attribute is used to identify the contents. Under these circumstances, a sub-vector with the names vector can be used in a similar way as the positive integral labels. The following examples will explain this concept:

```
> cars <- c(5, 10, 1, 20)
> names(cars) <- c("Toyota", "Ford",
"Mitsubishi", "Chevrolet")
>    foreign    <-    cars[c("Toyota",
"Mitsubishi")]
```

Character vectors are beneficial because alphanumeric names are usually easier to remember than numeric indices. It is an especially useful option for data frames. Indexed expressions can also be on the receiving end of an assignment, where the assignment is done only on the elements relevant to the vector. The expression must have the "vector[index_vector]" form. It must have random expression instead of the vector name.

The following example will clarify this point:

```
// Missing values are replaced in x
by                              zeros
>         x[is.na(x)]           <-      0
> y[y < 0] <- -y[y < 0]
```

```
// This example has the same effect
> y <- abs(y)
```

## Vector Arithmetic

Vectors maybe used in arithmetic expressions. Therefore, the mathematic operations are performed element by element. Vectors that occur within the same expression does not have to have the same length. If they do not, the value of the expression is a vector that has the same length as the longest vector within the expression. Short vectors within the expression are recycled as often as necessary until there is a match made with the longest vector. Specifically, when a constant is being repeated.

In the following example, the vector generates a vector "v"

of length 11. This is created by adding element by element, by using 2 * x, repeated 2.2 times, where y is repeated only once and one is repeated eleven times.

The basic arithmetic operators used with vectors are +, -, *, /, and ^.

```
> v <- 2*x + y + 1
```

Additionally, there are common arithmetic functions include log, exp, sin, cos, tan, sqrt, and others. These were mentioned earlier, but again, it is revisited to show the association of functions and vectors.

Here are some arithmetic functions that used with vectors:

- **Min() and Max()** - The min() and max() functions are used to select the smallest and largest elements within a vector. They select the largest and smallest values for their arguments, even if they have several vectors. The pmax() and pmin() function are equivalents to the min() and max() functions. They return a vector that is equal to the longest argument that contains the largest or smallest elements of the input vectors.

- **Range()** - The range() function usually has a vector of length two, for example c(min(x), max(x)).

- **Length(x)** – The length() function contains the

number of elements of x.

- **Sum(x)** – The sum() function provides the total number of elements in x.
- **Prod(x)** – The prod() function provides the product of x.
- **Mean()** – The mean() function calculates the sample mean. This is the same as sum(x)/length(x).
- **Var(x)** – The var() function calculates the sample variance, which is the same as sum()x-mean(x))^2)/length(x)-1. if the argument within var() is an n by p matrix, then the value is a p by p sample covariance matrix that was obtained by considering the rows as independent p-variate sample vectors.
- **Sort(x)** – The sort(x) returns a vector of the same size as x. The elements are arranged in ascending order. Other variations of the sort() function include order() and sort.list() functions. They are equivalents to the sort() function.

Typically, you should not be concerned if the values in a numeric vector are integers, complex numbers, or real numbers because internal calculations are performed as double precision real numbers or double precision complex numbers if the input data is complex.

When working with complex numbers, you should provide

an explicit complex part. Therefore, if you use sqrt(-17) it will return NaN and a warning. On the other hand, the following example will perform calculations with complex numbers.

```
> sqrt(-17+0i)
```

## Special Values

The readBin() and writeBin() functions passes missing and special values, but it should not be used if there will a size change. Missing values in R for logical and integer types is the "**INT_MIN**" type. It is the smallest integer that is defined the C header "limits.h". This normally corresponds to the bit pattern 0x80000000.

When special values are represented in R, numeric and complex types can be machine and compiler dependent. Therefore, the easiest way to use them is to connect them to an external application against the RMath library, which exports the double constants "**NA_REAL**", "**R_PosInf**", and "**R_NegInf**". You will also need to include the RMath.h header, which defines the macros "**ISNAN**" and "**R_FINITE**".

In R, characters that are missing values are written as NA, but there are no options to recognize character values as missing because this can be done through reassignment when they are read.

## Numerical Summaries

R includes several functions that are used to calculate numerical summaries. Some of these include the summary(), mean(), and var() functions. The list of statistical functions used for this purpose is extensive. They are primarily used for representing datasets numerically. If a dataset labeled "y" for instance, and the intention is to create a sequence from 1 to 50, you can use a variety of functions to return statistical results.

To assign the sequence 1 to 50 and call the list of numbers within the sequence, you would do the following:

```
>        y            <-          1:50
> y
```

The above statement would give you the following results:

```
[1]   1   2   3   4   5   6   7   8   9  10  11
12  13  14  15  16  17  18  19  20  21  22  23
[24]  24  25  26  27  28  29  30  31  32  33
34  35  36  37  38  39  40  41  42  43  44  45
46
[47]  47  48  49  50
```

You can use any of the following functions to achieve the appropriate numerical results:

- **max()** – The max() function provides the maximum number, for example:

```
>                                    max(y)
[1]  50
```

- **min()** – The min() function provides the minimum number, for example:

```
>                                    min(y)
[1]  1
```

- **mean()** – The mean() function provides the mean number, for example:

```
>                                    mean(y)
[1]  25.5
```

- **median()** – The median() function provides the median number in the sequence, for example:

```
>median(y)
[1]  25.5
```

- **sd()** – The sd() function provides the standard deviation of the sequence, for example:

```
>                                          sd(y)
[1] 14.57738
```

- **range()** – The range() function provides the range of the sequence, for example:

```
>range(y)
[1] 1 50
```

- **var()** – The var() function calculates the variance of the sequence, for example:

```
>var(y)
>[1] 212.5
```

- **sum()** – The sum() function calculates the sum of the sequence, for example:

```
>                                          sum()
>[1] 1275
```

- **fivenum()** – The fivenum() function

```
>                                     fivenum(y)
[1]   1.0 13.0 25.5 38.0 50.0
```

- **quantile()** – The quantile() function calculates the associated numbers defined in percentiles, for example:

```
> quantile(x,  c(.15,  .10,  .75,  1))
  15%        10%          75%        100%
  8.35   5.90 37.75 50.00
```

- **IQR()** – The IQR() function calculates the Interquartile range of numbers, for example:

```
>                                    IQR(x)
    [1] 24.5
```

- **which.min()** – The which.min() function returns the lowest element number within the sequence, for example:

```
>                            which.min(x)
[1] 1
```

- **which.max()** – The which.min() function returns highest element number within the sequence, for example:

```
>                            which.max(x)
[1] 50
```

# Text

## Text Processing

In this section, you will learn how to deal with strings in R. You will also learn about regular expressions and different ways that you use expressions to process simple and complex text, as well as how to perform statistical text analysis, collect data from unformatted text file, and manipulate character variables. Additionally, you will know how to read text files and how to use R functions with characters.

When processing text in R, there are actually two types of functions for characters that you can use. They are simple functions and regular expressions. Many of these functions are part of the R base package, which you will learn more about later on.

To locate the standard base R package, you would implement the following statement:

```
> help.search(keyword = "character",
package = "base")
```

## Reading and Writing Text Files

R allows you to read any text files with **"readLines()"** and **"scan()"** functions. You can specify the encoding for the imported text file with the readLines() function. All the contents of the text file can be read into an R object, for example a character scan. The scan() function on the other hand is more flexible. You can specify this type of data in the second argument.

```
// Assign and read text file
dataFile                          <-
readLines("textFile.txt",encoding="U
TF-8")
scan("textFile.txt", character(0))
```

```
// Each word is separated in the
file
scan("textFile.txt",    character(0),
quote = NULL)
```

```
// Quotes are removed from the file
scan("textFile.txt",    character(0),
sep = ".")
```

```
// Sentences are separated with a
new                                line
scan("textFile.txt",    character(0),
sep = "\n")
```

You can write the contents of an object into a text file by using the cat() or the writeLines() functions. The cat() function concatenates vectors by default you are writing to a text file. You can change it by implementing options such as **sep="\n"** or **fill=TRUE**. The default coding is based on the computer you are using.

In the following example, you will see how to implement the "**cat()**" and "**writeLines()**" to write a text file.

```
cat(text,
dataFile="textFile.txt",sep="\n")
```

or

```
writeLines(text,          con      =
"textFile.txt", sep = "\n", useBytes
= FALSE)
```

Before reading the contents of a file, you should evaluate the contents by using one of the following functions that is appropriate.

- **nlines()** – The nlines() is a parser package function that allows you to count the number of lines in a file.

223

- **countLines()** – The countLines() is a R.utils package function that counts the number of lines in a file.
- **count.chars()** – The count.chars() is parser package function that counts the number of bytes and characters for each line within a file.
- **file.show()** – The file.show() function is used to display text files.

## Character Encoding

R provides various functions with a different set of encoding schemes. This is necessary when you are working with text file that were created on another operating system and if was created in a language that is not English. They may have specific characters and accents that differ from the English language. For example, the standard encoding on a Linux OS is "UTF-8", but the standard encoding scheme for a Window system is "Latin1". The encoding() function in R, for example, returns the encoding string. The iconv() function is a similar function tot the command "incov" in Unix. They both convert the encoding.

Here is a list of some character encoding functions that are used in R:

- **iconvlist():** The "**inconvlist()**" function returns a list of encoding schemes on your computer.

- **readLines(), scan()** and **file.show():** These three functions also have encoding options.

- **is.utf8() {tau}:** The "**is.utf8() {tau}**" function tests if the encoding is "**utf8**".

- **is.locale() {tau}:** The "**is.locale()**" function tests to see if the encoding is the same as the default encoding on your computer.

- **translate() {tau}:** The "**translate() {tau}**" function is for converting the encoding to the current locale.

- **fromUTF8() {descr}:** The "**fromUTF8() {descr}**" function is not as general as the iconv() function.

- **utf8ToInt() {base}** : The "**utf8ToInt() {base}**" function is for converting to and from UTF-8 encoded character vectors.

> **Important:** You will need to include the "**{tau}**", "**{descr}**", and "**{base}**" packages to use the appropriate character encoding functions.

In the following "**Windows**" example, the default encoding is set to "**latin1**".

```
> texty      <-     "Some    Text"
> Encoding(texty)    [1]    "latin1"
>            texty1              <-
iconv(texty,"latin1","UTF-8")
> Encoding(texty1) [1] "UTF-8"
```

## Regular Expression

A regular expression is a structure that includes a set of strings. For example, you could have the following pattern – two numbers, two letters, and four numbers. R provides various functions for managing regular expressions. There are two types of regular expressions in R. They are extended regular expressions and Perl-type regular expressions. The following syntax demonstrates how they are implemented.

- **Extended regular expressions** – The "**perl = FALSE**" argument is the default.

- **Perl-type regular expressions** – The "**perl = TRUE**" argument the other format.

There is also another option. It is the "**fixed = TRUE**" argument. This is considered as a literal regular expression. You can also use the "**fixed() (stringr)**" function. It is the same as using the "fixed = TRUE"

226

argument in the standard regex functions. These functions are case sensitive by default, but you can change it by setting the "**ignore.case = TRUE**" option. If you are not an expert in regular expressions, you can use the "glob2rx()" function. The function means that you are suggesting that a specific regular expression has a specific pattern. The following expression demonstrates how this can be done.

```
> glob2rx("xyz.*") [1] "^xyz\\."
```

## Regular Expression Functions

The following functions are used with regular expressions:

- **sub(), gsub(), str_replace() {stringr}** – These are used to convert substitutions into a string.

- **grep(), str_extract() {stringr}** – These are used to extract a specific value.

- **grepl(), str_detect() {stringr}** – These are used to detect the existence of a pattern.

- **splitByPattern() {R.utils}** – This is used to split a single character string by pattern.

- **gsubfn()** - This is located in the gsubfn package. It can take a replacement function or a specific object.

> **Important:** You will need to include the "{stringr}" and "{R.utils}" packages to use the appropriate regular expression functions.

The following default expressions are considered extended regular expressions:

- **"."** – This means any character.
- **[ABC]** - This means A,B or C.
- **[A-Z]** - This means any uppercase letter between A and Z.
- **[0-9]** - This means any number between 0 and 9.

There is also a list of meta-characters. They include "$, *, +, . ,?, [ ], ^, { }, |, ( ), \". To use any of these characters, you will need to use the double backslash (\\) before them.

R also provides some classes of regular expressions for numbers, letters, characters, and for combining additional classes.

The following regular expression is used for implementing numbers:

- "[:digit:]" - This represents digits or numbers from 0 to 9 (0, 1, 2, 3, 4, 5, 6, 7, 8, 9).

The following regular expressions are used for implementing letters:

- [:alpha:] – This is used to implement alphabetic characters, which includes uppercase ([:lower:]) and lowercase letters ([:upper:]).
- [:upper:] - This is used to implement uppercase letters.
- [:lower:] – This is used to implement lowercase letters.

> **Note:** Alphabetic characters may include accents, for example é è ê, which is common in languages such as French and Spanish. Therefore, it is more general than upper and lowercase letters used in the English language, which does have many accents.

The following regular expressions are used for implementing specific characters:

- [:punct:] - This is for implementing these punctuation characters: "!, ", #, $, %, &, ', (, ), *, +, ",", -, ., /, :, ;, <, =, >, ?, @ [, \, ], ^, _, `, {, |, }, ~,".

- **[:space:]** - This is for implementing the space characters: tab, newline, vertical tab, form feed, carriage return, and space.
- **[:blank:]** – This is for implementing the blank character; space and tab.
- **[:cntrl:]** - This is for implementing control characters.

The following regular expressions are used for implementing a combination of classes:

- **[:alnum:]** - This is for implementing alphanumeric characters. The "**[:alpha:]**" and "**[:digit:]**" is used with this expression where appropriate.
- **[:graph:]** – This is for implementing graphical characters. The "**[:alnum:]**" and "**[:punct:]**" is used with this expression where appropriate.
- **[:print:]** – This is for implementing characters that you can print. The "**[:alnum:]**", "**[:punct:]**", and "**[:space]**" is used with this expression where appropriate.
- **[:xdigit:]** – This is for implementing the hexadecimal digits "0 1 2 3 4 5 6 7 8 9 A B C D E F a b c d e f".

To count the number of repetitions, you could add any of the following characters after the regular expressions:

- **?** – The "?" character is optional and will match only once when implemented.
- **\*** - The "*" character will 0 or more number of times.
- **+** - The "+" character will match one or more number of times.
- **{n}** - The "{n}" expression will match "n" number of times. This means any number that represents "n".
- **{n,'}** – The "{n,'}" expression will match "n" or more number of times.
- **{n,m}** – The "{n,m}" expression will match at least "n" number of times, but it cannot match more than "m" number of times.
- **^** - The "^" character is used to force the regular expression to the beginning of the string.
- **$** - The "$" character is used to force the regular expression to end of the string.

To learn more about these characters, enter the following two help files in the command line of R:

```
// This expression provides some
general                 information.
>?regexp
```

231

```
// This is used to retrieve help
file for grep(), regexpr(), sub(),
etc
>?grep
```

You can also use regular expressions that is "Perl-type", for example you can use the "**perl = TRUE**" argument in the sub() function to remove character strings. You would add the double backslash (\\) Perl-type macro to actually remove the space characters in a string. The following example will show you how to do it.

```
> sub('\\s', '',y, perl = TRUE)
```

# Text Manipulation

R allows you to manipulate text using different functions, packages, and methods. In this section, you will learn different ways on how to manipulate character strings and numbers. Many of these functions are stored in built-in R packages that you will need to include when you create the functions.

## String Concatenation

In R, string concatenation is accomplished by using one following functions:

232

- **paste()** – The "**paste()**" function concatenates strings.

- **str_c() {stringr}** – The "**str_c() {stringr}**" function also concatenates strings in a similar way to the paste() function.

- **cat()** – The "**cat()**" function prints and concatenates strings.

> **Important:** You will need to include the "**{stringr}**" package to use "**str_c()**" function.

The following examples will show how the "**paste()**", "**str_c()**", and "**cat()**" functions are used to concatenate strings:

```
// Paste() - A space is used to
separate the text to concatenate.
>    paste("work","load",sep='    ')
[1] "work load"
```

```
// Paste() - A comma (,) is used to
separate the text to concatenate.
>       paste("work","load",sep=",")
[1] "work,load"
```

```
// Str_c() - A comma (,) is used to
separate        the        text.
>        str_c("work","load",sep=",")
[1] "work,load"
```

```
// Paste() - A space is created with
the        "collapse"        argument.
>    x    <-    c("we","are","young")
>      paste(x,      collapse="    ")
[1] "we are young"
```

```
// Str_c() - A space is created with
the "collapse" argument.
> str_c(y, collapse = " ")
[1] "we are young"
```

```
// Cat() - The "+" operator is used
to  concatenate  three  characters.
>  cat(c("x","y","z"),  sep  =  "+")
[1] x+y+z
```

## Splitting Strings

R uses the **"strsplit()"**, **"string_split(){stringr}"** and **"tokenize() {tau}"** functions to split strings. Here is some additional information about these functions:

- **strsplit()** - The **"strsplit()"** function splits the element within a character vector 'x' into substrings. This is based on the matches made to split the strings within the substring. The "str_split() (stringr)" function is also used to split the strings within the substring. The following example shows how the function is used to split character strings.

```
// strsplit() splits x.y.z character
string.
>    unlist(strsplit("x.y.z",    \\.))
[1] "x" "y" "z"
```

- **tokenize() {tau}** – The "**tokenize() {tau}**" function splits the strings into tokens. The following example shows how the "tokenize()" function can be used to split strings into tokens.

```
// The tokenize() function splits
the character string "xyz abcdef"
>        tokenize("xyz        abcdef")
[1] "xyz"     " "         "abcdef"
```

**Important:** You will need to include the "{stringr}" and "{tau}" packages to use the string_split() and tokenize() functions.

## Counting Strings

The "**nchar()**" and "**str_length() {stringr]**" functions returns the length of a string.

- **nchar()-** The "nchar()" function returns the length of a string. You can also use the "str_length()(stringr) as an alternative to obtain the length of a string. Here are some examples of how the nchar() and  function can be used to obtain a string length.

```
//   The   nchar()function   returns   a
numeric  string  length  for  "wxyz".
>                      nchar("wxyz")
[1] 4
```

```
// The str_length() function returns
the    numeric    string    length    for
"wxyz".
>                 str_length("wxyz")
[1] 4
```

```
// The nchar() function returns the
numeric   string   length   for   "STR".
>                        nchar(STR)
[1] 3
```

```
//The str_length() function returns
the   character   string   for   "STR".
>                    str_length(STR)
[1] STR
```

> Important: You will need to include the "{stringr}" package to use the str_length() function.

## Pattern Detection

Pattern detection is evaluated with the "**grepl()**" and "**str_detect()(stringr)**" functions.

- **grepl()-** The grepl() function returns a logical expression "TRUE" or "FALSE".

- **str_detect() {stringr}** – The str_detect()(stringr) function is the alternative function for pattern detection.

The following examples shows implements the grepl( ) and str_detect() functions to determine if a pattern is "TRUE" or "FALSE".:

```
// Example 1: Two strings are assigned.
> string1 <- "07 Nov 1973"
> string2 <- " 4 Nov 1971"
```

```
// The grepl() function returns TRUE
for                           "string1".
>    regexp    <-    "([[:digit:]]{2})
([[:alpha:]]+)        ([[:digit:]]{4})"
>    grepl(pattern    =    regexp,    x    =
string1)
[1] TRUE
```

```
//The str_detect() function returns
TRUE           for           "string1".
>     str_detect(string1,     regexp)
[1] TRUE
```

```
// Example 2: grepl() returns FALSE
for                           "string2"
>    grepl(pattern    =    regexp,    x    =
string2)
[1] FALSE
```

In the first example, "TRUE" is returned because all "digits" and "alpha" are correct, but the second example returns "FALSE" because the first digit only returns 1 number.

**Important:** You will need to include the "**{stringr}**" package to use the grepl() function.

## Counting Pattern Strings

The "**textcnt()**" function counts the occurrence of patterns within a string.

- **textcnt() {tau}** – The "textcnt() **{tau}**" function counts the occurrence of each pattern or each term within a string. The following example uses the textcnt() function to count the pattern strings.

```
> string1 <- "November 07 bday 1973
April        4        bday        2015"
>
textcnt(string,n=1L,method="string1"
) November      bday        07       4
attr(,"class")
[1] "textcnt"
```

> **Important:** You will need to include the "**{stringr}**" packages to use the textcnt() function.

## Substring Position Extraction

The "**cpos() {chimisc}**" and "**substring.location() {cwhmisc}**" functions are used to return a specific position in the substring.

- **cpos() {cwhmisc}** – The "**cpos() {cwhmisc}**" function returns the position of a substring in a string.
- **substring.location() {cwhmisc}** – The "substring.location() **{cwhmisc}**" function performs

the same as the "cpos() {**cwhmisc**}" function, but it returns the first and last position in a string.

```
// The number position for letter
"p" is returned. Counting starts at
the         letter         "a".
>
cpos("abcdefghijklmnopqrstuvwxyz","p
",start=1)
[1] 16
```

```
// The number position for the first
and last letter of the "def" string
is                          returned
>
substring.location("abcdefghijklmnop
qrstuvwxyz","def")
> $first [1] 4   > $last [1] 6
```

**Important:** You will need to include the "{**cwhmisc**}" package to use the "**cpos()**" and "**substring.location()**" functions.

## String Position Extraction

The "**regexpr()**" function returns a specific position in a string.

- **regexpr()** – The "**regexpr()** returns the position of a regular expression.

- **str_locate() {stringr}** – The "str_locate() {**stringr**}" function performs the same task as the "**regexpr()**" function.

- **gregexpr()** – The "gregexpr(" is similar to the regexpr() function, but the starting position of every match found is returned.

- **str_locate_all() {stringr}** – The "str_locate_all() (**stringr**)" also performs the same task as the other functions.

```
> regexp <- "([[:digit:]]{2})
([[:alpha:]]+) ([[:digit:]]{4})"
> string <- "myname 23 day 2015
myname 18 day 1971"
> regexpr(pattern = regexp, text =
string)
```

```
[1] 8 attr(,"match.length")

[1] 11
```

```
> gregexpr(pattern = regexp, text =
string)
[[1]]
[1] 8 27 attr(,"match.length")
[1] 11 11
```

```
>          str_locate(string,regexp)
start   end   [1,]              8      18
>          str_locate_all(string,regexp)
[[1]]           start end [1,]      8    18
[2,]      27   37
```

> **Important:** You will need to include the "{stringr}" package to use the "str_locate()" and "str-locate_all()" functions.

## Substring Extraction

The "**substr()**" and "**str_sub() {stringr}**" functions are used to extract a substring from a string. You can extract a fixed width substring using one of these functions.

- **substr()** - The "substr()" takes a sub string from a string.

- **str_sub() {stringr}** – The "str_sub() {stringr}" function performs the same way as the "substr()" function.

The following example implements the "**substr()**" and "**str_sub()**" functions:

```
// The first and second character of
the        string       is        returned
>          substr("some          text",1,2)
[1] "so"
```

```
>          str_sub("some          text",1,2)
[1] "so"
```

**Important:** You will need to include the "**{stringr}**" package to use the "**str_sub()**" function.

## Word Extraction

The "first.word()" function is used to extract the first word in a string.

- **first.word(){hmisc}** – The "**first.word(){hmisc}**" function extracts the first word or expression.

The following example will show you how to use the "**first.word()**" function.

243

```
// The first word in the string is
returned.
> first.word("Extract First Word")
[1] "Extract"
```

> **Important:** You will need to include the "{hmisc}" package to use the "**first.word()**" function.

## Extract String Pattern

The "**grep()**" function is used to extract a string pattern.

- **grep()** - The "grep()" returns the value or the position of the regular expression if "value=T" and if "value=F".

The following examples show to implement the grep() function to return a value or position of an expression:

```
//The grep() function returns the
pattern of a string
> grep(pattern = regexp, x = string1
, value = T)
[1] "07 Nov 1973"
```

```
// The grep() function returns the
position        of        the        string
> grep(pattern = regexp, x = string2
,    value    =    T)        character(0)
> grep(pattern = regexp, x = string1
,            value            =            F)
[1] 1
```

```
> grep(pattern = regexp, x = string2
, value = F)   integer(0)
```

R also provides the following function to extract specific strings:

- **str_extract(), str_extract_all(), str_match(), str_match_all() (stringr) and m() {caroline}** – These functions are similar to the grep()function.

- **str_extract() and str_extract_all()** - The "str_extract() and str_extract_all()" functions will return a vector.

- **str_match() and str_match_all()** - The "str_match() and str_match_all()" functions will return a matrix and m() function dataframe.

245

The following examples will show you how to use each of these functions:

```
// A string is assigned with the
day, month and year.
> library("stringr")
>    regexp    <-    "([[:digit:]]{2})
([[:alpha:]]+) ([[:digit:]]{4})"
> string1 <- "November 07 bday 1973
November 22 2015"
```

```
// The str_extract() function is
implemented to extract a specific
string
>         str_extract(string,regexp)
[1] "07 November 1973"
```

```
// The str_extract_all() function is
implemented to extract the entire
string.
>    str_extract_all(string1,regexp)
[[1]] [1] "07 Novemver 1973" "22
November 2015"
```

```
// The str_match"() function is
implemented to match a specific
string.
>           str_match(string,regexp)
> [,1]               [,2] [,3]   [,4]
[1,]  "07  November  1973"  "22"
"November" "2015"

// The str_match_all() function is
implemented to match the entire
string.
>        str_match_all(string,regexp)
[[1]]         [,1]              [,2] [,3]
[,4]   [1,] "07 November 1973"  "07
November                        1973"
[2,]  "22  November  2015"  "22"
"November" "2015"
```

```
// The m() function is implemented
to match the day, month, and year.
> library("caroline")
```

```
> m(pattern = regexp, vect =
string1,         names         =
c("day","month","year"),  types  =
rep("character",3))  day month year
[1] 22   November 2015
```

## String Substitution

R allows you to make a string substitution within a string. The following functions below are used interchangeably to make substitutions.

- **sub()** – The "**sub()**" function is the standard function for making a string substitution within a string.

- **gsub()** – The "gsub()" performs the same way as the sub() function. The only difference is the gsub() function replaces all occurrences of the pattern, whereas the sub() only replaces the first occurrence.

- **str_replace() {stringr}** – The "**str_replace() {stringr}**" function also has the same functionality as the sub() and gsub() functions.

> **Important:** You will need to include the "{stringr}" package to use the "str_replace()" function.

In the following example, the British date is used with the pattern 2 digit day, blank space, letters, a blank space, and a 4 digit year. The 2 digit day is detected with the "[[:digit:]]{2}" expression, the letters are detected with the "[[:alpha:]]+" expression, and the 4 digit year is detected with "**[[:alpha]]+**" expression. The three strings are within a set of parenthesis. The first substring is saved in "\\1", and the second substring is saved in "\\2" and the third substring is saved in "\\3".

```
// The first substring returns the
first part of the regular
expression.
> string <- "07 November 1973"
> regexp <- "([[:digit:]]{2})
([[:alpha:]]+) ([[:digit:]]{4})"
> sub(pattern = regexp, replacement
= "\\1", x = string)
```

```
// The second substring returns the
second part of the regular
expression.
> sub(pattern = regexp, replacement
= "\\2", x = string)
```

```
// The third substring returns the
third part of the regular
> sub(pattern = regexp, replacement
= "\\3", x = string)
```

In the following examples, the "**sub()**" and "**gsub()**" functions are used to replace strings. The first example uses the sub() function to remove the first space and the second example uses the gsub() function to remove all the spaces in the string.

```
// The sub() function removes the
first    space    in    the    string
> textString <- "sub string rep"
> sub(pattern = " ", replacement =
"",           x    =    textString)
[1] "substring rep"
```

```
// The gsub() function removes all
the    spaces    in    the    string.
> gsub(pattern = " ", replacement =
"",           x    =    textString)
[1] "substringrep"
```

## Character Substitution

The "**chartr()**" function allows you to substitute characters in an expression or statement. The definition of the function means "**character translation**". You can also use the following functions to perform the same task as the "**chartr()**" function.

- **replacechar(){cwhmisc}** – The "**replacechar(){cwhmisc}**" function is in the {cwhmisc} package. It is also used to substitute characters in an expression.

250

- **str_replace_all(){stringr}** – The "**str_replace_all(){stringr}**" function is in the {stringr} package. It performs the same task as the "**chartr()**" and "**replacechar()**" functions.

The following examples will show you how to substitute characters with chartr(), replachcar(), and str_replace_all() functions:

```
// The chartr() function replaces a
single                   character.
>  chartr(out="y",  in="a",x="myth")
[1] "math"
```

```
// The chartr() function replaces a
string         of         characters.
>
chartr(out="yth",new="aths",x="myth"
)
[1] "maths"
```

```
// The replacechar()replaces unique
characters     in     the     string.
>
replacechar("count.the.digits.now","
.","_")
[1] "count_the_digits_now"
```

```
// The str_replace_all() replace all
unique characters in the string.
>
str_replace_all("count_the_digits_no
w","\\_",".")
[1] "count.the.digits.now"
```

**Important:**   Remember  to  include  the
"{cwhmisc}" and "{stringr}" functions to use the
replacechar() and str_replace_all() functions.

## Convert Letters

R allows you to convert letters in various ways. You can
use one of the following functions to perform the
appropriate letter conversion:

- **tolower()** - The "**tolower()**" function converts
  uppercase to lowercase letters.
- **toupper()** – The "toupper()" converts lower-case to
  upper-case letters.
- **capitalize() {hmisc}** – The "**capitalize()**" function
  in the {hmisc} package capitalizes the first letter of
  a string.
- **cap(){cwhmisc}** – The "**cap()**" function performs
  the same task as the toupper() function, by
  capitalizing letters.

- **capitalize(){cwhmisc}** – The "**capitalize()**" function performs the same task as the cap() and toupper() functions.

- **lower(){cwhmisc}** – The "**lower()**" function performs the same task as the tolower() function, by converting uppercase to lower-case letters.

- **lowerize(){cwhmisc}** – The "lowerize()" function performs the same task as the tolower() and lower() function, by converting uppercase to lowercase letters.

- CapLeading(){**cwhmisc**} – The "CapLeading()"function capitalize the first character in a string.

The following example will show you how to apply the "**tolower()**", "**toupper()**", and "**capitalize()**" functions.

```
// The tolower() function converts
upper case letters to lower case
letters.
>              tolower("FLorida")
[1] "florida"
```

```
// The toupper() function converts
lower case letters to upper case
letters.
>              toupper("FLorida")
[1] "FLORIDA"
```

```
// The captialize() function
converts the first letter from lower
case to upper case letter. It
applies the title case.
>            capitalize("florida")
[1] "Florida"
```

> **Important**: Remember to include the "{**hmisc**}" and "{**cwhmisc**}" packages to use the appropriate letter conversion function.

## Character Fill

Characters are filled in a string with the "**padding()**" function with specific characters of set length. The "**str_pad()**" is also used to fill characters in a string. The following examples applies the padding() and str_pad() functions to fill characters in a string.

```
// Blank spaces are used to make the
length of string 10. Characters are
set            to          the          right.
>            library("cwhmisc")
>    padding("abc",10,"    ","right")
[1] "        abc"
```

```
// The "*" character is used to fill
the         blank         spaces.
>      str_pad("abc",      width=10,
side="right",      pad      =      "*")
[1] "***xyz****"
```

```
//Leading "0" are set to the left of
each digit character to fill the
blank spaces if the character digit
is       less       than       2.
>
str_pad(c("1","2","8","10"),2,side="
left",pad="0")
[1] "01"   "02"   "08"   "10"
```

The "**str_pad()**" function operates very slowly, for example, if you have a 1000 length vector, it would take a long time to compute it. The "**padding()**" function on the other hand, handles character vectors in better way, but the best way is to use both the "sapply()" and "padding()" functions. The following examples show how you can implement the str_pad(), padding(), and sapply() functions.

```
//   Include   the   "stringr"   and
"cwhmisc"   package   and   assign   the
character                    vectors.
>library("stringr")
```

```
>library("cwhmisc")
>a <- rep(1,10^4)
```

```
//The str_pad() function computes
the processing time - takes a long
time.
>           system.time(b          <-
str_pad(a,3,side="left",pad="0"))
user         system            time
50.968   0.208        73.322
```

```
//  The  sapply()  and  padding()
functions  are  used  together.  It
takes a shorter time to process than
the                        str_pad().
>   system.time(c   <-   sapply(a,
padding, space = 3, with = "0", to =
"left"))
      user         system            time
     7.700    0.020        12.206
```

**Important:** Remember to include the "**{stringr}**" and "**{cwhmisc}**" package to use the applicable functions.

## Remove Spaces

R provides the "trimws() {memisc}", "trim(){gdata}", and "str_trim(){stringr} functions to remove    leading and trailing white spaces. The following examples will show you how to use them:

```
// The trimws() function removes
leading and trailing white spaces.
>                library("memisc")
> trimws("    two   vectors        ")
[1] "two vectors"
```

```
// The trim() function does the same
job  as   the   trimws()   function.
>                library("gdata")
>    trim("    two    vectors       ")
[1] "two vectors"
```

```
// The str_trim() function also does
the  same  job  as  the  trim()  and
trimws()                   functions.
>            library("stringr")
> str_trim("     two   vectors      ")
[1] "two vectors"
```

**Important:** Remember to include the "{memisc}", "{gdata}" and "{stringr}" packages to use the functions for removing leading and trailing white paces.

## Compare and Compute Strings

R provides specific operators and functions for assessing and comparing strings. The following examples will show you each these functions and operators are applied.

- **==** - The "==" operator returns TRUE if both of the strings are the same and FALSE if it is not. It is used to determine if the strings are the same.

```
// The expression returns "FALSE".
>                    "xyz"=="zyz"
[1] FALSE
```

```
// The expression returns "TRUE".
>                    "xyz"=="xyz"
[1] TRUE
```

> **Note:** The functions that are used compare and calculate strings apply to the Levenshtein distance. This is a string metric function that is used for measuring the distance between two strings.

- **adist() {utils}** — The "adist()" function of the {utils} package is used to calculate the approximate string distance between vectors.

258

```
>          adist("match","matching")
[1]  3
```

- **stringMatch(){MiscPsycho}** – The "stringMatch()" function in the {MiscPsycho} package is used to compare the similarity of two strings. If "normalize = YES" in the function, then the "Levenshtein distance" is divided by the maximum length of the string.

```
//   The   stringmatch()   function
returns   the   number   of   characters
that         do         not         match
>              library("MiscPsycho")
>
stringMatch("match","matching",norma
lize="NO",penalty=1,case.sensitive =
TRUE)
[1]  3
```

- **stringdist() {stringdist}** - The "stringdist()" function in the {stringdist} package returns an approximate string matching and string distance.

```
// The stringdist() function returns
the number of characters that do not
match.
>              library(stringdist)
>        stringdist("live","lively",
method="dl")
[1]  2
```

259

- **levenshteinDist(){RecordLinkage}** – The "levenshteinDist()" function in the {RecordLinkage} package compares two strings.

```
// The levenshteinDist() function
compares          two        strings.
levenshteinDist("records","recrd")
```

The **"agrep()"** function may also be used to approximate matches the Levenshtein distance. The following expressions are used within function to return the value of the string.

- **"value = TRUE"** – The "value=TRUE" expression returns the value of the string.
- **"value = FALSE"** – The "value=FALSE" expression returns the position of the string.
- **max** – The "max" expression returns the maximal Levenshtein distance.

The following examples implements the **"agrep()"** function to return the value of a string:

```
>    agrep(pattern = "lively", x =
c("1 live", "1", "1 LAZY"), max = 2,
value           =            TRUE)
[1] "1 lazy"
```

```
>   agrep("lively", c("1 live", "1",
"1 LIVE"), max = 3, value = TRUE)
[1] "1 lazy"
```

There are also some miscellaneous functions that are used to manipulate and evaluate string expressions.

- **deparse()** – The "**deparse()**" function converts unevaluated expressions into character strings.

- **char.expand() {base}** – The "**char.expand() {base}**" function expands a string based on its target.

- **pmatch() {base}** and **charmatch() {base}** – The "**pmatch() {base}** and **charmatch() {base}**" function are used to search for matches within the elements of the first argument.

The following example implements the "**pmatch()**" and "**nomatch()**" functions:

```
// The pmatch() function returns "0"
if      there      is      "nomatch".
>         pmatch(c("w","x","y","z")
> table = c(("x","z")nomatch = 0)
[1] 0 1 0 2
```

- **make.unique()** – The "**make.unique()**" function is used to make a unique character string. This will help you to turn a string into an identifier.

261

The following example applies the "**make.unique()**" function to make a string into an identifier:

```
// The make.unique() function makes
each          character          unique
>   make.unique(c("x",   "x",   "x"))
[1] "x"    "x.1" "x.2"
```

**Note:** Remember to include the "**{base}**" package to use the char.expand(), pmatch(), and charmatch() functions.

# Text Processing Functions

When processing text in R, you may find that you do not remember the name of a function or how to apply a function's usage. It is helpful to have an easily accessible reference to built-in text processing functions. You can use this section as a point of reference for these functions.

## String Functions

Strings are the same as character vectors in R, but a character vector in other programming languages are considered an array of strings. You will learn more about how string functions are applied in the following examples:

```
// The str() function evaluates
"textword"
>        str      =        "textword"
> str[1]
```

If you would access individual characters within an R string, you will need to use the "**substr()**" function(). The first argument in the substr() function is considered a character vector, the second is the index for the first character you need, and the third is the index for the last character you need.

```
// The substr() function evaluates
"t"              in         "textword"
>     str        <-         "textword"
> substr(str, 1, 1)
```

> **Note:** If you would like to find the number of characters within a string, do not use the length() function, use the nchar() function instead.

The following example shows another way that you can use the substr() function:

```
// The substr() function locates
positions 1 and 2 and 7 and 8 in the
string.
>     str     <   -        "textword"
>     substr(str,  1,  2)     ==   "te"
> substr(str, 7, 8) == "rd"
```

Notice that the substr() function allows you to access single characters within the string by using an indexing method. If you would like to break the strings into vectors of characters, you will need to use the strsplit() function. It works similar to the split() function that is used in Perl. The following example will explain how it works:

```
// The strsplit() function evaluates
a                                    list
> strsplit('0-0-1', '-')
```

## Paste Function

In the previous section, you learned about splitting strings apart, but you will also need to know how to put the characters into strings. You can accomplish this with the paste() function. It is a strange function that is used for concatenating strings in R, but it is also used to perform tasks associated with the join() function used Perl.

The following example will show you how the function works:

```
// A space is added to the output
>       str1        <-        "string1"
>       str2        <-        "string2"
> print(paste(str1, str))
```

In the above example, you will notice that there is a space added with the "str" argument. A space is added because the paste() function carries an optional argument for a separator when joining strings that defaults to a single space. The following example will provide some clarification:

```
// The paste() function includes a
separator
> paste("string1", "string2") ==
paste("string1", "string2", sep ="
")
```

To remove the space, you will need to use a null separator.
The following example uses the print() and paste()
together to accomplish this task:

```
> print(paste("string1", "string2",
sep = " "))
```

## Case Conversion

In an earlier section, case conversion was discussed.
However, to further understand how it is used in text
processing, you will need to learn more. As mentioned
earlier, the tolower() and toupper() functions are used to
change letters from uppercase letters to lowercase and the
reverse, but you can also use them with the substr()
function to convert the commonly used words into a title
case form.

The following example will show you how to combine the
toupper() and the substr() function to return a string with
only uppercase title letters:

```
>          pseudo.titlestring          <-
function(str)
>     {    subset    str,    1,    1)    =
toupper(substr(str,        1,      1))
> return(str)  }
```

## Translate Characters

To translate characters, you can use the chartr() function. This was also discussed in an earlier section. The chartr() function translates characters that is inputted into related characters of your choice. The following example will show you how to use the chartr() function to evaluate a string.

```
// The chartr() function evaluates
the                              ABC
> chartr("xyz", "ABC", "xyzxyz")
```

If you are a Perl programmer, you will recognize the similarity to the "tr()" function.

## Substring Containment

If you would like to learn how to contain a string into another string or a set of strings, you will need to apply the charmatch() function that was used in an earlier example.

267

In the following example, the charmatch() function is used to contain a substring.

```
// The charmatch() function returns
0
> charmatch("w", c("mean", "mode"))
```

```
// The charmatch() function returns
2
>    charmatch("med",    c("mean",
"median"))
```

**Note:** Regular expressions are generally used instead of substring matching, therefore it may not be necessary to use the charmatch() function.

**Tip!** If you would like to use more complex text processing, you may want to use regular expressions and the grep() functions. If necessary, you can implement approximate expression matching system with the Levenshtein distance method.

# Data Frames

Data frames are a list that contains the "data.frame" class. In R, there are certain restrictions placed on lists in data frames. Here is a list of restrictions that you should be aware of:

- The components must be vectors of type numeric, character, logical, factors, numeric matrices, lists, or other data frames.

- You can have as many variables to the data frame as columns, elements, or variables.

- Numeric vectors, logical vectors, and factors are as is. Character vectors must be vectors with unique vectors inside the vector itself.

- Vector structures that are variables in the data frame must have the same length. The structure of the matrix must have the same row size.

- A data frame can be considered a matrix with columns that have different modes and attributes. They may look like a matrix and have row and columns that were removed with the matrix index conventions.

# Data Frame Objects

Data frames that are used in R are similar to the Statistical Analysis System (SAS) and Statistical Package for Social Sciences (SPSS) data set. They are used to store information. It allows you to take several different types of vectors and save them in a variable. Vectors used in data frames may include various lists with factors, strings and numbers. They behave similar to a matrix.

Overall, a data frame consists of a list of vectors, factor, and various matrices with the same length. When referring to matrices, they have the same number of matrices. Data frames also have a names attribute for labeling variables. The **"row.names"** attribute for labeling cases of variables.

A data frame may contain a list that is same as other components. The list may have elements with different lengths, which provides a form of data structure for ragged arrays.

Objects that are used to fulfill restrictions on columns or components of a data frame can be used to create a data frame with the **"data.frame()"** function.

The following example will show you how to create a data frame with the **"data.frame()"** function:

```
>              results              <-
data.frame(grade=classgrade,
subject=course, age=avgage)
```

A list that contains contents that satisfies the restrictions of a data frame can be forced into a data frame with the data.frame() function. The easiest way to initially create a data frame is with the read.table() function. It allows you to read a complete data from frame from an external file. You will learn more how to do this in the following section.

## Creating Data Frames

You can create and manipulate data frames in many different ways. Here is an example that will show you how to create a data frame:

```
// Contents for the data frame is
created
>       x        <-        c(1,2,3,4)
>       y        <-        c(2,4,6,8)
>            Products            <-
factor(c("X","Y","X","Y"))
```

```
//Data frame is created with three
columns
> results <- data.frame(first=x,
second=y,                z=products)
>                          results
first       second                z
1       1       2 etc...
```

```
// The contents of the data frame is
returned
B > summary(results)
first           second      z
Min.   :1.00  Min.   :2.0   A:2
1st Qu.:1.75    1st Qu.:3.5      B:2
etc...
```

```
// Contents of the first column is
returned
>                     results$first
[1] 1 2 3 4
```

```
//Contents of the second column is
returned
>                     results$second
[1] 2 4 6 8
```

```
//Contents of the third column is
returned
> results$f
```

```
[1] A B A B

Products:  A B
```

Data frames allow you to manipulate data in various ways. In the following sections, you will learn different ways that you can manipulate data within a data frame.

## Rename Columns

To rename the columns in a data frame you should start by creating a sample data. In following example you will learn how to do this.

```
// Data frame with three columns of
sample data is created
biz      <-      data.frame(invest=1:3,
buy=4:6, sell=7:9)
[1] invest buy sell
       1    4    7
       2    5    8 etc...
```

```
//    The    columns    are    returned
>                              names(biz)
[1] "invest" "buy"   "sell"
```

The best way to rename the columns is to use the rename() function in the {plyr} package.

```
// The rename() function renames the
"invest"    and    "sell"    columns
  > rename(biz, c("invest"="money",
"sell"="save"))
  money          buy                save
    1             4                  7
    2             5                  8
    3    6        9
```

You do not have to depend on the **{plyr}** package, instead you can modify the variable. The following example incorporates built-in functions and modifies the "**biz**" variable used in the above example. You will see that you do not have to save the results in the "**biz**" variable.

```
// The names() function renames the
"invest"    column    to    "money"
>    names(biz)[names(biz)=="invest"]
<-                    "money"
  money              buy          sell
    1                 4             7
    2    5        8 etc...
```

```
// The names() function renames the
column by index: The "sell" column
is        renamed        to        "save"
names(biz)[3]        <-        "save"
    money        buy        save
    1        4        7
    2    5    8 etc...
```

You can also use the search and replace function in R to rename columns. The caret "^" and "$" operators in following example is to ensure that the all the characters in the string matches. If you do not have them, then another column with a similar name would match, and the replacement would be incorrect.

The following example will show you how to use these operators to make the appropriate changes:

```
// The "^" and "$" are implemented.
> names(biz)    <-    sub("^invest$",
"money",                names(biz))
    money        buy        save
    1        4        7
    2    5    8 etc...
```

```
//All occurrences of the letter "s"
are replaced with "R" in all
columns.
> names(biz) <- gsub("s", "r",
names(biz))
money               buy              Rave
     1                4                 7
     2    5        8 etc...
```

In the above example, the "**gsub()**" function replaces all the occurrences of the letters in each column. If you use the sub() function on the other hand, it replaces only the first occurrence of within each column name.

## Add and Remove Columns

If you would like to add or remove columns from a data frame, there are many different ways that you can do this. The following example will show you how to do this.

```
//A data frame with two columns is
created
data    <-    data.frame    (id=1:3,
products=c(20,27,24))
  code products
    1      20
    2      27
    3      24
```

```
// Different ways to add a column
```

```
data$category             <-  c("new",
"used", "recycled")
data[["category"]]    <-    c("new",
"used", "recycled")
```

```
data["category"]          <-  c("new",
"used", "recycled")
data[,"category"]         <-   c("new",
"used", "recycled")
data$category       <- 0
```

```
// Different ways to remove a column
data$category        <- NULL
data[["category"]] <- NULL
data["category"]     <- NULL
```

```
data[,"category"]   <- NULL
data[3]            <- NULL
data[,3]           <- NULL
data                    <-  subset(data,
select=-category)
```

## Reorder Columns

In the following example, you will learn how to reorder columns in a data frame:

277

```
// A data frame is created with
three columns - "code" "products"
"category"
> data <- data.frame (code=1:3,
products=c(20,27,24),category=c("new
", "used", "recycled"))
```

```
//The original order of the columns
code          products          category
  1              20                 new
  2              27                used
  3      24      recycled
```

```
// The columns are reordered by
number.
>                       data[c(1,3,2)]
  code   category       products
   1        new         20
   2        used        27
   3   recycled      24
```

```
//      Change   the   actual   data.
> data <- data[c(1,3,2)]
```

```
// Reorder the column by name
>      data[c("category",    "code",
"products")]
```

| category | code | products |
|----------|------|----------|
| new | 1 | 20 |
| used | 2 | 27 |
| recycled | 3 | 24 |

The above examples are indexed into the data frame by handling it like a list. The data frame is actually a list of vectors, which can be used like a matrix. The following example will show you how this is done using the data[row, col] argument.

```
//Creating  a  list  similar  to  a
matrix
> data[, c(1,3,2)]
```

| code | category | products |
|------|----------|----------|
| 1 | new | 20 |
| 2 | used | 27 |
| 3 | recycled | 24 |

One of the setbacks of matrix indexing is that it produces different results when you specify a single column. Under these circumstances, the object that is returned is a vector and not a data frame. The returned data type is not always consistent with matrix indexing. Therefore it is better that you use the list-style indexing.

The following examples will show you both list-style and matrix-style indexing:

```
// List-style indexing with a single
column
>                              data[2]
products
       20
       27
       24
```

```
//  Matrix-style  indexing  with  a
single column
data[,2]
   20
   27
   24
```

## Merge Data Frames

To merge two data frames into a single column, you would use something like the **"join"** keyword in SQL. The following example:

```
// A data frame mapping is created
with "bookname".
```

```
> bookname <- read.table(header=T,
text='bookid   title 1 investment 2
poetry 3 humor ')
```

```
// A data frame is created with book
numbers.
>            booknumbers          <-
read.table(header=T,    text='subject
bookid rating   1    1    6.7   1  2
4.5  1  3    3.7            2     2
3.3  2  3    4.1   2  1    5.2 ')
```

```
// Merge the two data frames
>      merge(book,  data,  "bookid")
     bookid subject rating  bookname
       1       1    6.7    investment
       1       2    5.2       poetry
       2       1    4.5       humor
etc...
```

If you have two data frames with different for the columns that you would like to match, you must specify the names. The following example will show you how to do this.

```
// The column name "bookcode" is
used     instead    of    "bookid".
>   book2   <-   read.table(header=T,
text='     bookcode          bookname
```

```
1        investment    2      poetry
3        humor ')
```

```
// The "bookid" and "bookcode"
column merge.
> merge(x=bookname, y=booknumbers,
by.x="bookid", by.y="bookcode")
  bookcode  bookname subject rating
     1       investment  1     6.7
     1        poetry     2     5.2
     2        humor      1     4.5
```

Notice that the column name is inherited from the first data frame (bookname).

You can also merge multiple columns with data frames. The following example will show you how to do this:

```
// Additional book titles are added
to the data with the read.table()
function
> titlename <- read.table(header=T,
text='   size type        computer
programming  sales business fiction
health  relationship  non  fiction
medicine           certification
gardening religion ')
```

```
>          bookdescription          <-
read.table(header=T,          text='
number    size   type                1
investment    computer              2
poetry    business            3 humor
relationship 4    investment    health
')
```

```
// The two data frames are merged.
> merge(bookdescription, titlename,
c("size","type"))
```

```
    size type number        name
    investment        computer       1
investment
    poetry    business          4 humor
relationship
```

## Compare Data Frames

To compare two or more data frames and locate rows in more than one data frame or rows you can use data frames to accomplish this task.

In the following example, there are there data frames that will locate each row from each data frame. It will show you how each data frame appears in at least one data frame.

```
// A data frame with two columns are
created - "Topic" and "Answer"
>                  data                <-
data.frame(Topic=c(1,1,2,2),
Answer=c("Y","Y","Y"))
```

```
Topic Answer
Y
Y
Y
```

```
dataB <- data.frame(Topic=c(1,2,3),
Answer=c("Y","N","Y"))
 Topic Answer
   1       Y
   2       N
   3       Y
```

```
dataC <- data.frame(Topic=c(1,3,4),
Answer=c("N","Y","N"))
 Topic Answer
   1       N
   3       Y
   4       N
```

In the "**data**" data frame, the rows that contains "**1, Y**" also appears in the data frame "**dataB**". However the rows that have "**2, Y**" does not occur in any of the other data frames.

The same is true for the "**dataB**" data frame that contains "**3, Y**", which also appears in the "**dataC**" data frame, but "**2, N**" does not appear in any other data frame.

> **Note:** You may want to check repeated or unique rows data in another data frame.

## Join Data Frames

R also allows you to join data frames. In the following example, you will see how to join three data frames with a column that identifies the source of each row. The column in the data frame is called "**dataSymbol**" It represents the data that could be used by three different persons. Under these circumstances, you may want to locate where the "**dataSymbol**" match, or where they do not match.

```
// Columns are created
data$Symbol <- "A"
dataB$Symbol <- "B"
dataC$Symbol <- "C"
```

```
// Combine the columns
ds <- rbind(data, dataB, dataC)
```

```
//Reorder columns for appearance
df <- df[,c(3,1,2)]
```

```
// Display columns
 Symbol Topic Answer
    A      1     Y
    A      1     Y
    A      2     Y
```

| B | 1 | Y |
|---|---|---|
| B | 2 | N |
| B | 3 | Y |

| C | 1 | N |
|---|---|---|
| C | 3 | Y |
| C | 4 | N |

If you use this format for your data, it is recommended that you join them together.

## Find Duplicate Rows

The function "**dupsBetweenGroups()**" used in the following example is used to help you find replicated rows between different groups.

```
// Locate the rows from different
groups that have duplicates.
repRows                          <-
dupsBetweenGroups(ds,"Symbol")
```

```
//Display the rows with data frame
with the data frame
>cbind(ds, rep=repRows)
 Symbol    Topic    Answer    rep
    A        1         Y      TRUE
    A        1         Y      TRUE
    A        2         Y      FALSE
```

| | | | |
|---|---|---|---|
| B | 1 | Y | TRUE |
| B | 2 | N | TRUE |
| B | 3 | Y | FALSE |

| | | | |
|---|---|---|---|
| C | 1 | N | FALSE |
| C | 2 | Y | TRUE |
| C | 3 | N | FALSE |

The above example does not really point to duplicated rows within the set. With the "Symbol = A" for example, you will notice that there are two rows with "Topic = 1" and "Answer = Y". They are not marked as duplicates, though.

## Find Unique Rows

You can also use data frames to find rows that are unique within a set.

```
// Set unique rows
> cbind(ds, Valid=!repRows)
```

| Symbol | Subject | Response | Valid |
|---|---|---|---|
| A | 1 | Y | FALSE |
| A | 1 | Y | FALSE |
| A | 2 | Y | TRUE |

| | | | |
|---|---|---|---|
| B | 1 | Y | FALSE |
| B | 2 | N | FALSE |
| B | 3 | Y | TRUE |

| | | | |
|---|---|---|---|
| C | 1 | N | TRUE |
| C | 3 | Y | FALSE |
| C | 4 | N | TRUE |

## Split Data Frame

In this section, you will learn from the following examples how to split a joined data frame using the data frames that were created earlier.

```
// Save the results in the "ds"
variable
> dsRep <- cbind(ds, Rep=repRows)
```

```
//Splits all the rows with the
Symbol "A".
> data <- subset(dsRep, Symbol=="A",
select=-Symbol)
```

| Topic | Answer | Rep |
|---|---|---|
| 1 | Y | TRUE |
| 1 | Y | TRUE |
| 2 | Y | FALSE |

```
// Splits all the rows with the
Symbol "B".
```

289

```
dataB <- subset(dsRep, Symbol=="B",
select=-Symbol)
```

| Topic | Answer | Rep |
|-------|--------|-------|
| 1 | Y | TRUE |
| 2 | N | TRUE |
| 3 | Y | FALSE |

```
// Splits all the rows with the
Symbol "C"

dataC <- subset(dsRep, Symbol=="C",
select=-Symbol)
```

| Topic | Answer | Rep |
|-------|--------|-------|
| 1 | N | FALSE |
| 2 | Y | TRUE |
| 3 | N | FALSE |

## Ignore Columns

R also allows you to ignore one or more columns in a data frame. This is accomplished by removing the column that is passed to the function from the data frame. When the results are returned, you can join to complete the data frame, if necessary.

```
// Ignore the "Topic" column and use
only the "Answer" column.
```

```
dNoColumn  <-  subset(ds,  select=-
Topic)
```

| Symbol | Answer |
|--------|--------|
| A      | Y      |
| A      | Y      |
| A      | Y      |

| | |
|---|---|
| B | N |
| B | Y |
| B | N |

| | |
|---|---|
| C | N |
| C | Y |
| C | N |

```
// Check for any repeated rows
repRows                          <-
dupsBetweenGroups(dsNoColumn,
"Symbol")
```

```
// Combine the results to the
original data frame
> cbind(df, rep=repRows)
```

```
//Display the results
```

| Symbol | Topic | Answer | Rep |
|--------|-------|--------|------|
| A      | 1     | Y      | TRUE |
| A      | 1     | Y      | TRUE |

| | | | |
|---|---|---|---|
| A | 2 | Y | TRUE |

| | | | |
|---|---|---|---|
| B | 1 | Y | TRUE |
| B | 2 | N | TRUE |
| B | 3 | Y | TRUE |

| | | | |
|---|---|---|---|
| C | 1 | N | FALSE |
| C | 2 | Y | TRUE |
| C | 3 | N | FALSE |

The "**dupsBetweenGroups()**" function is responsible for doing all the work to get the desired results.

## Recalculate Columns

R allows you to recalculate the factor levels for columns in a data frame. Sometimes you will need to recalculate columns because you may have factor columns that have specific levels that are no longer necessary.

In the following example, "**d**" data frame has one blank row. When you read into it, the factor levels have an empty space (" "). This should not be in the data.

```
d <- read.csv(header = TRUE, text='
x, y, value a,one,1 ,, b,two,4')
d
```

```
x       y value
a     one       1

                5
b     two       4
```

## Vapply() and Lapply()

To recalculate all the levels of factor columns, you will need to use the "vapply()" and the "lapply()" functions. The "vapply()" function is used with the "is.factor()" function to determine which columns are factors. The "lapply()" function is then used to apply the "factor()" function to the columns.

```
// Determine which columns are
factors.
>       factor_cols    <-    vapply(d,
is.factor, logical(1))
    x      y value
  TRUE   TRUE FALSE
```

```
// The factor() function is applied
to the column
d[factor_cols]                      <-
lapply(d[factor_cols], factor)
```

```
str(d)
```

```
// Data frame with three variables
 $ x        :  Factor  w/  3  levels
"a","b","c": 1 2 3
 $ y        :  Factor  w/  3  levels
"one","three",..: 1 3 2
 $ value: int  1 4 10
```

## Evaluate Columns

The "**colwise()**" function from the {plyr} package is used to implement a function to each of the columns in the data frame. The function will be able to determine if the column is either a factor or normal vector. If the column has a factor, the "**factor()**" function is used to remove the unused levels, but it if it is a normal vector, the vector will not change.

The following example will show you how you to implement the "**colwise()**" and "**factor()**" function.

```
// The {plyr} package accesses the
colwise() function.
library(plyr)
```

The factor object is determined with the function. If it is a factor object, then the "factor()" function is implemented. The function is used to recalculate the factor levels or return the unchanged vector. The following statements illustrate how this is done.

```
refactor_factor <- function(col)
{    if (is.factor(col))  factor(col)
else col }
```

When the "**factor()**" function is applied, it will remove the unused levels.

```
// Levels a, b, and c
refactor_factor(d$x)
[1] a b c
```

```
// An unchanged vector is returned
for a non-factor vector.
refactor_factor(d$value)
# [1]  1  4 10
```

Since the "**refactor_factor()**" function is implemented in the above example, the colwise() function is now applied to all the columns in the data frame.

The "**colwise()**" function returns a function and then apply the "**refactor_factor()**" function to all the columns in the object that is passed to it.

```
// The colwise() function applies
the "refactor_factor()" function.
d <- colwise(refactor_factor)(d)
str(d)
```

```
'data.frame':        3  obs.  of    3
variables:
 $  x          :  Factor  w/  3  levels
"a","b","c": 1 2 3
 $  y          :  Factor  w/  3  levels
"one","three",..: 1 3 2
 $ value: int   1 4 10
```

## Attach() and Detach()

If you use the "$" notation in a variable, for example
**"results$school"**, to list contents or components may not
be suitable. It would be better to make the components of a
list or data frame briefly visible as variable within the
component name. You do not need to refer to the list name
specifically.

The "**attach()**" function will allow you to use the
"database", for example a list or data frame, as the
function's argument. If grades are in a data frame for
example with two variables, "**grades$a**" and "**grades$b**",
then you could use the attach() function by doing the

following:

```
> attach(grades)
```

The "**attach()**" function allows you to place the data frame in the search path of the second position if there are no variables, a, b or c in position. In the following example, a, b, and c are variables from the data frame.

```
> a <- b+c
```

The above assignment does not change the "**a**" component of the data frame, but instead covers it up with another variable "**a**" within the directory at the first position of the search path. If you would like to permanently make changes to the data frame, the easiest way is to implement the "$" notation. The following example will show you how to do this:

```
> grades$a <- b+c
```

In the above expression, the new value of component "a" will not be visible until the data frame is detached and reattached. To detach the data frame, use the "**detach()**" function.

```
> detach()
```

When you implement the detach() function, it will detach

from the search path for the element in the second position. Therefore, the variables a, b, and c would no longer be visible, unless the notation is specified as "**grades$a**". The elements greater than the second position on the search path can be detached by providing a number, but it is better to use a name, for example "**detach(grades)**" or "**detach("grades")**".

> **Note:** R allows lists and data frames to be attached at the second position or greater. Whatever is attached is considered a copy of the original object. You can change the attached values by using the "**assign()**" function, but bear in mind that the original list or data frame will remain the same.

## Working With Data Frames

Data frames are a useful for working with different problems within the same directory. If you would like to efficiently work with data frames, you will need to do the following:

1. Bring all the variables together for specific problems in a data frame and assign an appropriate name.
2. When working with problem, ensure that you attach

the appropriate data frame for the second position and then use the working directory at the first level for usable quantities and temporary variables.

3. Before you leave a problem, ensure that you add any variables that you would like to keep for future reference to the data frame with the "$" operator and then use the "**detach()**" function.

4. The last thing that you should do is to remove all the unnecessary variables from the working directory. Make sure that you remove as many temporary variables. When you do this, it makes it easier to work with many problems in the same directory that have the variables, a, b, and c, for example.

## Attach() Arbitrary Lists

The attach() function is generic and allows directories and data frames to be attached to the search path. However, other object classes are also attached in the same way, specifically any object with the object mode "list".

The following example shows how the "**attach()**" function works with lists:

```
> attach(any.old.list)
```

> **Note:** Any elements that were attached, can be detached using the detach() function, by the position number or by the name.

## Manage Search Path

The "**search()**" function in R is used to show the current search path. It can be helpful when you are trying to figure out which data frames, lists, and packages that are attached or detached.

When you enter the "search()" function at the R command line, you will get something that looks like the following:

```
>                            search()
[1]                        ".GlobalEnv"
"tools:rstudio"      "package:stats"

[4]                   "package:graphics"
"package:grDevices" "package:utils"
```

The "**.GlobalEnv**" expression in the above example specifies the workspace. If "**grades**" are attached, you may get the something that looks like the following:

300

```
>                             search()
[1]    ".GlobalEnv"           "grades"
>                             ls(2)
[1] "a" "b" "c"
```

Notice that the "ls()" function or objects can be used to evaluate the contents of any position within the search path. The last thing that you should do is to detach the data frame and confirm that it has been removed from the search path.

In the following example, the "detach()" function is implemented to detach "grades" from the search path.

```
>                        detach("grades")
>                             search()
[1]    ".GlobalEnv"         "Autoloads"
"package:base"
```

```
"package:base"

"Autoloads"
"package:base"
```

# Matrix and Arrays

Matrices and arrays are similar, but they are used to manipulate and handle data in different ways. In this chapter, you will learn how to create and manipulate arrays and matrices for different scenarios and special cases.

## Arrays

An array is a collection of multiple data entries, for example numeric and characters. R provides options for creating and managing arrays, as well as other special types of matrices.

In R, a dimension vector is considered a vector of non-negative integers, whose length can be n. If the length is n, then the array is n-dimensional; for example a matrix that has a two dimensional array. The dimensions in the array are indexed from one to the values that is in the dimension vector. A vector can also be used by R as an array if the dimension vector has the dim attribute. If a vector for example, has 1000 elements, the expression would look like the following example:

```
> dim(y) <- c(2, 5, 100)
```

The above example uses the dim attribute, which applies a 2 by 5 by 100 array. You can use the matrix() and array() functions as alternative solutions to make the expression simple and more natural. The values in the data vector provide an array that looks similar to the ones in FORTRAN. They appear in a column-like format with the first subscript moving the quickest and last subscript moving the slowest.

If the dimension vector for an array "**x**" is c(2, 3, 5), then it would have 2 * 3 * 5 = 30 entries in "**x**" and the vector would have the order x[1, 1, 1,], x[2, 1, 1] ... x[2, 3, 4], x[2, 3. 5].

Arrays that are one-dimensional are treated the same as vectors. This includes printing.

## Array Indexing

You can reference individual elements of an array by providing the name of the array with subscripts. The subscripts are written in the square brackets and separated by commas.

Arrays have subsections that are specified with a sequence of index vectors instead of subscripts. However, if an index position has an empty index vector, the entire subscript is adopted.

In reference to the previous example, "a[a,,]" with a 4 by 2 array that has a dimension vector c(4.2) and data vector that contains the following values:

```
>   c(a[2,1,1],   a[2,2,1],   a[2,3,1],
a[2,4,1],
    a[2,1,2],    a[2,2,2],    a[2,3,2],
a[2,4,2])
```

The above example has the format "a[,,]", which stands for a complete that is the same as removing the subscripts completing and implementing "**a**" independently. If you an array, for example "A", the dimension vector can be implemented exclusively as "**dim(a)**". You can reference if from both sides.

If you provide the array name with a single subscript or index vector, the values that are associated with the data vector are used. If this is case, the dimension vector is not recognized. If the single vector is not a vector array, then it does apply.

## Array() Function

In addition to providing a vector structure with a dim attribute, arrays can be created from vectors with the **"array()"** function with the following format:

```
Z <- array(data_vector, dim_vector)
```

If you have a vector **"a"** for example and it contains 16 or less numbers, then the expression may look like the following:

```
> Z <- array(a, dim=c(2,4,2)
```

This example could be could use **"a"** to create a 2 by 4 by 2 array in Z. If the size of **"a"** is the same as 16 then the result would be the same as the following example:

```
> Z <- a ; dim(Z) <- c(2,4,2)
```

On the other hand, if **"a"** is shorter than 16 and the values are recycled from the start and goes up to size 16 and you use something like the following example, you would receive a mismatch error for the length, because **"S"** is not a designated array.

```
> dim(S) <- a(2,4,2)
```

As an alternative, you could use the following example:

```
// Makes "Z" an array with all zeros
> Z <- array(0, c(2,4,2))
```

In the above example, dim(Z) means that there is a dimension vector of c(2,4,2). The "**Z[1:16]**" argument means the data vector in "a", along with Z[] and an empty subscript or Z without any subscripts. This means it is a complete array.

You can use arrays in arithmetic expressions and the result is an array that operates on an element-by-element basis on the data vector. The operands for the dim attributes need to be the same, which becomes the dimension vector for the results. Therefore, if you have X, Y, and Z arrays that similar, you would implement something like the following example:

```
> D <- 2*X*Y + Z + 1
```

The above example is the "D" array that has a data vector that performs an element-by-element operation. It is a mixed array with vector calculations. There are specific rules surrounding the calculations of mixed arrays and vectors. The exact rule will be discussed in more detail in the following section.

## Index Matrices

Index vectors with subscripts are similar to matrices and can be used with a single index matrix. They can assign vector with quantities to unbalanced elements in an array or extract unbalanced elements as a vector.

Using a matrix example will make it is easier for you to understand. If you have double index array, you can provide an index matrix with two columns with as many rows as you would like. The entries in the index matrix include the row and column indices for the double index array. If you have a 4 by 4 array called "B" for example, you would extract the elements B[1,3], B[2.2] and B[3,1] as vector structure. You could then replace the inputs in the "B" array with zeroes.

If you do this, you could use a 3 by 2 subscript array. The following examples will show you how to do this:

```
// A 4 by 4 array is created
> B <- array(1:20, dim=c(4,4))
>                               B
 [,1]   [,2]           [,3]        [,4]
91317 101418 111519 121620
```

```
[1,]    1   5
[2,]    2   6
[3,]    3   7
[4,]    4   8
```

```
// A 3 by 2 index array is
implemented.
> i <- array(c(1:3,3:1), dim=c(3,2))
> i
```

```
//Displays elements for 3 by 2 array
       [,1] [,2]
[1,]    1   3
[2,]    2   2
[3,]    3   1
// Extract the specified elements
>                               B[i]
[1]          9          6          3
> B[i] <- 0 > B

// Replace the elements with zeros
       [,1] [,2] [,3] [,4]
[1,]    1   5
```

```
[2,]     2     0
[3,]     0     7 etc...
01317 101418 111519 121620
```

You are not allowed use negative indices in index matrices. However, NA and zero values are allowed. The rows in the index matrix ignore the zeros and uses "NA" to return non-applicable results. If you would like create a minimally designed matrix for a block design with blocks (b levels) and varieties (v levels) factors. Additionally, you can do this if you have "n" plots in the test. The following example will show you how to do this.

```
// Omit the zeros
> Bx <- matrix(0, n, x)
> By <- matrix(0, n, y)
```

```
// Create the elements for "x"
and "y"
> ix <- cbind(1:n, blocks)
> iy <- cbind(1:n, varieties)
```

```
// Combine the elements for "x"
and "y"
> Bx[ix] <- 1
> By[iy] <- 1
```

```
> B <- cbind(Bx, By)
```

You can construct the incidence matrix. For example if you have a matrix "**D**", you could do the following:

```
> D <- crossprod(Bx, Bz)
```

There is also an easier way to implement this matrix. You could use the table() function by doing the following:

```
> D <- table(blocks, varieties)
```

It is important to note that index matrices must be numerical and if a logical or character matrix is used for example, the matrix is treated an index vector.

## Mixed Vectors and Arrays

The specific rule that affects element-by-element mixed calculations with vectors and arrays can be somewhat complicated. It is recommended that use the recycling rule as a guide to help you perform better calculations with vectors and arrays. The recycling rule states the following:

- The expression should be assessed from left to right.
- Short vector operands are extended by recycling their value until they match the size of other operands.
- When short vectors and arrays are met, the

310

arrays must have the same dim attribute. If not an error will occur.

- When a vector operand is longer than a matrix or an array, an error will occur with the operand.

When there is an array structure and the vector does not have an error, then the result is an array with the dim attribute with the array operands.

## Outer Product of Arrays

One of the most important operation is calculating the outer product of two array. For example, if you have "x" and "y" array, then the outer product is an array that has a dimension vector resulting from the concatenation of two dimension vectors, and the data vector is obtained by creating the products of all the elements of the data vector of arrays "x" and "y". The outer product is created by the "%0%" operator.

This is how you could implement this special operator.

```
> fg <- f %o% g
```

You could also use the following alternative method:

```
> fg <- outer(f, g, "*")
```

In the above example, the multiplication function is replace by the outer function that has two variables. If you would like to evaluate the function $f(x:y) = \cos(y)(1 + x^2)$ on a grid with "x" and "y" coordinates that is specified in R by vectors "x"and "y", you could implement the following expressions:

```
> a <- function(x, y) cos(y)/(1 +
x²)
> b <- outer(x, y, a)
```

Notice that the outer part of the two regular vectors is a double subscripted array. This is a matrix that has position of one at the most. Also, notice that the outer product operator is independent.

If you have the determinants of a 2 by 2 matrices "[a, b; c, d]", where each element is a non-negative integer that ranges from 0 to 9, you would need to find the determinants, ad, bc, for all the possible matrices. You could also represent how often each of the value occurs as a high-density plot. This would result in the probability distribution of the determinant for each digit, if they are selected independently and randomly.

You could do this by implementing the "**outer()**" function two times. The following example will show you how to do this:

```
// The outer() function specifies
the elements of a 2 by 2 matrix.
> prod <- outer(0:9, 0:9)
> num <- table(outer(prod, cnt, "-
"))
```

```
// The "Determinant" and the
"Frequency" is specified.
> plot(as.numeric(names(num)), num,
type="a",
        xlab="Determinant",
ylab="Frequency")
```

In the above example, notice that the coercion of the names attribute for the "Frequency" table is set to numeric to retrieve the range of determinant values. The best way to do this is by using for loops.

## Transpose Array

To rearrange or transpose an array is by implementing the "aperm()" function. The syntax is specified as follows:

```
> aperm(a, perm)
```

The above example rearranges an array "a". The argument

313

"perm" must be a permutation of integers {1,......k}, where k is number of subscripts for the array "a". The function returns an array with the same size as the array "a", but has the dimensions provided by "perm[ j ]", which becomes the new j-th dimension. The best way to seeing this operation is by considering it as a generalized way to transpose matrices.

If you a matrix "X" with a double subscript array, then you could have matrix "Y" be expressed as follows:

```
> Y <- aperm(X, c(2,1))
```

In this case, you could use a less complex function. You could use the transpose function ("t()") to simplify the expression.

Here is how you could use the t() function to transpose the matrix "X".

```
>Y <- t(X)
```

## Matrices

Matrices are two dimensional data structures that contain elements with the same data types. Data types for a matrix may include numeric, logical, character, or complex. You can use the matrix() function to create a matrix that may look like the following example:

```
// A matrix that uses the integers 1
to 12 in 3 rows and 4 columns
> matrix (1:10, mrow = 4, mcol = 3)
```

```
        [,1]        [,2]        [,3]
[1,]      1          5           9
[2,]    2    6    10 etc...
```

You do not have to define both "mrow" and "mcol" arguments because R assumes the other once one is given. Notice that the data is based on a column-by-column basis, unless you define another row. If you create the "**byrow=N**" argument for example, the matrix may look like the following:

```
> matrix (1:12, mrow = 4, byrow = N)
          [,1] [,2] [,3]
[1]       1    2    3
[2,]      4    5    6 etc...
```

Please take note of this matrix example, because it will be used in future matrix examples.

```
y <- matrix (1:12, mrow = 4,
byrow=N)
> dim(y)
```

The above example has a matrix with a 4 by 3 dimension. Also notice that the vector has a length of 2.

315

## Matrix Columns

Columns in matrices must have the following format: **"mode(numeric, character, etc)"** with the same length. The standard format may have the syntax that looks similar the following:

```
> mymatrix <- matrix(vector, mrow=r,
mcol=c,                      byrow=FALSE,

carnames=list(char_vector_rownames,
char_vector_colnames))
```

The "**byrow = TRUE**" argument indicates the matrix should have rows, whereas the "**byrow=FALSE**" argument indicates that the matrix should have columns, which is by default. The "carnames" argument provides optional labels for columns and rows in the matrix.

The following examples show how these columns and rows are created:

```
// Creates 5 x 4 numeric matrix
y<-matrix(1:20, nrow=5,ncol=4)
```

316

```
> cells      <-      c(1,26,24,68)
> rnames   <-   c("Row1",   "Row2")
> cnames <- c("C1", "C2")
mymatrix   <-   matrix(cells,   nrow=2,
ncol=2,                      byrow=TRUE,
carnames=list(rnames, cnames))
```

The following example identifies specific rows and columns with subscripts.

```
// The 4th column of the matrix
y[,4]
```

```
// The 3rd row of the matrix
y[3,]
```

```
// Specifies rows 2, 3, and 4 and
columns     1,      2,      and      3.
> y[2:4,1:3]
```

## Matrix Construction

You can construct a matrix in different ways. You can construct a matrix by using data elements. This method will allow you to fill the content into the columns by default. For example, if you would like to create a matrix called "**X**" and fill the columns sequentially, you would create a matrix that looks like the following example:

```
> X = matrix(
    c(2, 4, 3, 1, 5, 7),
    nrow=3,
    ncol=2)
```

```
// The "X" matrix has 3 rows and 2 columns
> X
```

```
       [,1] [,2]
[1,]    2    1
[2,]    4    5 etc...
```

## Matrix Subscripts

When you have a vector, you can subscript with a single index. It is normal for you to use two subscripts for a matrix; you only need to separate them with a comma. The following example will show you how to do this:

```
// Three rows and two columns are specified.
> y[3,2]
[1] 8
```

```
// The result is a 3 by 2 matrix.
```

```
> y[1:3, c(1,3)]
>        [,1] [,2]
[1,]   1    3    etc...
```

When you omit a subscript, you will get an entire row or column. The following examples show how this is done.

```
> y[3,]
[1]  7  8  9
```

```
> y[,2]
[1]  2  5  8 11
```

The results that you see in the above examples are actually vectors. They are not matrices with a single row or column. If you ask for a two columns, then you will get a matrix. A matrix would look something like the following example:

```
>y[,c(1,3)]
        [,1] [,2]
 [1,]   1    3
 [2,]   4    6
 [3,]   7    9
```

If you wanted to, you could request one column or two, so it could continue being a matrix. You could do this by applying the **"drop=F"** argument. This is not used quite often, only to make it complete. The following example will guide you on how to do this:

```
// This is 1 by 3 matrix.
> y[2,,drop=F]
     [,1] [,2] [,3]
[1,]   4    5    6
```

```
// This is 4 by 1 matrix
> y[,2,drop=F]
              [1,]
      [,1]    2
    2 [2,]    5
    5 [3,]    8
```

## Combining Matrices

Two matrices that have the same columns and rows can be combined to create a larger matrix. For example, if you have a matrix called "**Y**" with three rows, you would combine matrix "X".

The following examples create matrix "**Y**" and combine matrix "**X**".

```
// A 3 by 1 matrix ("Y") is created
```

```
> Y = matrix(
    c(7, 4, 2),
    nrow=3,
    ncol=1)
```

```
// Matrix "Y" displays 3 rows
  > Y
```

```
        [,1]
[1,]     7
[2,]     4
[3,]     2
```

To combine matrix "X" with matrix "Y" you would use the "**cbind()**" function.

```
> cbind(X, Y)
        [,1]               [,2] [,3]
[1,]     2     1     7
[2,]     4     5     4
[3,]     3     7     2
```

The "**cbind()**" function allows you to combine the rows for the two matrices if you have the same number columns. You can also use the rbind() function to combine matrices. The following example will show you how to do this:

```
// A 6 by 2 matrix is created
Z = matrix(
```

```
    c(6, 2),
    nrow=1,
    ncol=2)
```

```
// The "Z" matrix has two columns
> Z
         [,1] [,2]
    [1,]  6    2 etc...
```

```
// The rbind() function combines
matrix    "X"    and    matrix    "Z"
> rbind(X, Z)
         [,1] [,2]
[1,]    2    1
[2,]    4    5 etc...
```

## Logical Subscripts

Just like with vectors, you can use logical vectors to select specific rows or columns. Typically, you can select a logical vector with one entry for each row. The same is also true for columns, for example, if you have the statement "**y[,2] > 5**", you would get the following results:

```
> y[,2] > 5
[1] F F T T
```

The above example has four entries, one entry for each row. If you wanted to only have rows and have the second

322

column greater than five (y[2] > 5, you could use the following example:

If we wanted only the rows for which the second column is > 5, we could do that simply:

```
// Provide specific rows and all the
columns
> y[y[,2] > 5,]
       [,1] [,2] [,3]
[1,]   7    8    9
[2,]   10   11   12
```

## Logical and Character Matrices

Here are some examples that will show you how to create logical and character matrices:

```
// This is a logical matrix
> y > 5
```

```
       [,1] [,2] [,3]
[1,]   F    F    F
[2,]   F    F    T
[3,]   T    T    T etc...
```

```
// A logical matrix that removes
values greater than five.
> y[y>5]
[1]  7 10  8 11  6  9 12
```

323

The above example actually returns a vector and a not a matrix. The process removes values column-by-column.

The following example is a character matrix that uses twenty-six letters in order.

```
// The quotes determine that they
are letters.

> matrix (letters[1:12], mrow = 4,
newrow = N)
```

```
     [,1] [,2] [,3]

[1,] "a"  "b"  "c"

[2,] "d"  "e"  "f"

[3,] "g"  "h"  "i" etc...
```

## Matrix Functions

In addition to the transpose function, there are also other functions that are used with matrices. Here is a list of those functions:

- **crossprod() function** – The crossprod() function is defined as "crossproducts" and has the syntax crosspro(X, y). This is same as having t(X) %*% y. The operator used in this instance is the multiplication operator, which you will learn more about. The second argument in the function is removed since the first one is used. It is considered to be the same as the first.

- **diag() function** – The diag() function is based on the argument on the inside of the function. For example, if you have the function diag(v), v defines the vector and provides a diagonal matrix with elements of the vector for diagonal entries. If you have diag(M) on the other hand, M is defined as a matrix, where the vector of diagonal entries belong to matrix M. Another convention is If you have diag(k), k is defined as the identity matrix.

One of the most widely used matrix function is the "t()" function. It transposes the matrix into the form "%*%". It also performs multiplication. The "solve()" function on the other hand inverts a matrix and solve linear systems.

The "transpose()" function transposes a matrix by interchanging the columns and rows of the matrix. If you have a matrix "X" for example, you would something like following:

```
//              Transpose              "X"
> t(X)

      [,1] [,2] [,3]
[1,]    2    4    3
[2,]    1    5    7
```

Here are some additional examples that will show you how the "**t()**" function and ,"**%*%**" operator works when transposing a matrix.

```
// The t() function transposes y
   > t(y)
```

```
     [,1] [,2] [,3] [,4]
[1,] 1    4    7    10
[2,] 2    5    8    11 etc...
```

```
// The t() function transposes y
number of times
t(y)
%*% y
```

```
      [,1] [,2] [,3]
[1,]  166  188  210
[2,]  188  214  240 etc...
```

```
// Unable to invert matrix using
this method
> solve (t(y) %*% y)
```

The "**solve()**" function allows you to solve simple and complex linear equations.

You could solve linear equations by using one of the following methods:

```
// Examples of linear equations
y = 2x +1
5x = 6 + 3y
y/2 = 3 - x
```

However, you can use the "**solve()**" function to solve the above example in R. The following example will show you how to create a matrix system called "equate" and produce a vector result called "result". The system will read as follows: "**(equate) y = result**". The next step is to find y by using the "solve()" function to invert the matrix. You would multiply the matrix by "result" or by calling the "**solve()**" function with the "equate" and result arguments.

```
// A four column matrix is created
with several numbers
> result <- c(2,2,3,3)
> equate <- matrix (c(14, 8, 16, 6,
5, 3, 7, 6, 5, 4, 3, 1, 2, 4, 7, 9),
ncol=4)
```

```
> solve (equate)
        [,1]                [,2]       [,3]
[,4]
[1,] -0.1511111   0.06   0.2288889  -
0.17111111
```

```
[2,]     0.5688889  -0.52  -0.3911111
0.40888889 etc...
```

```
// The solve() function implements a
4 x 1 matrix
> solve (equate) %*% result
```

```
          [,1]
[1,] -0.008888889
[2,]  0.151111111
[3,]  0.186666667 etc...
```

```
// The result is a vector of length
4
> solve (equate, c(2, 2, 3, 3))
[1]     -0.008888889        0.151111111
0.186666667  0.217777778
```

A matrix can be considered as an array with two subscripts. There are various operators and functions that are available in R for only matrices. The transpose function t() for example, is the matrix transpose function that is exclusively used for transposing matrices. There are also other functions, such as nrow() and ncol() functions. They nrow() function provides the number rows in a matrix and the ncol() function provides the columns in a matrix. If you have for example, nrow(X), you would get the number of rows in matrix X and if you have ncol(X), you would get the number of columns in the matrix X.

## Matrix Multiplication

As previously mentioned, the special operator %*% is used for matrix multiplication. If you have an "**m by 1**" or a "**1 by m**" matrix, you can use it as an m-vector if it is appropriate. Vectors in matrix multiplication expressions are automatically promoted to either row or column vectors, if it makes sense multiplicatively.

If matrix X and matrix Y are square matrices that have the same size, then "**X * Y**" is the matrix with element-by-element products. The matrix product would be "**X %*%**", and if there is a vector then the expression would be "**y %*% X %*% y**". This is the quadratic form.

## Row and Column Names

One thing that is really useful in R, is the option to name column and rows for your matrix. For example, if you have a set of columns called "y" with the names of cars and a set of rows for colors, your matrix would something like the following:

```
>   carnames(y)    <-   list   (c("Toyota",   "Ford",
"Honda", "Mitsubishi"), c("Black","White","Blue"))
```

Notice that the "**carnames()**" function creates a list. The first item on the list is a vector with a row of names and the second is a vector with column names. You can commit either the row or column and replace the vector with the "NULL" reserved word. The column "y" may look similar to following results.

```
// Display row and columns for the
carnames() function
> y
```

```
            Black White Blue
Toyota        1     2    3
Ford          4     5    6
Honda         7     8    9
Mitsubishi   10    11   12
```

You can now extract by name instead of by number. This is helpful because the numbers can change, for example you can remove specific rows or columns.

The following example will show you how you can remove a specific column:

```
// The top left column is returned
> y["Toyota","Black"]
```

```
[1] 1 > x[,"Black"]
```

```
// The "Black" column returns a
vector of names.
          Toyota        Ford        Honda
Mitsubishi
     Black    1        4      7      10
```

## Deconstruct Matrix

You can deconstruct matrix by implementing the c()
function. It is used to combine all column vectors in one.
The following example will show you how to do this:

```
// The c() function deconstructs the
"X" matrix.

> c(X)
[1] 2 4 3 1 5 7
```

# Dates

There are several options in R for handling date and date/time data. The built-in "as.Date()" function handles the dates without the times. The chron package is for handling dates and times, but does not handle time zones. There are also the "POSIXct" and "POSIXlt" classes for handing data and times with control over time zones. The rule when working with data and time data in R is to use the simplest method. Therefore, if you are handling date only data, you should use the as.Date() function. This is considered the best option. If you are handling both date and times without time zone information, you should use the chron package. The POSIX classes are best when manipulating time zones.

> **Note:** If you would like to convert data types use the "as." functions.

All the dates are stored internally as the number of days or seconds according to the reference date. However, the POSIXlt class does not have the facility. Therefore, dates in R are handled numerically and the class function is used to determine how they are stored. The POSIXlt class stores

333

the values for the date and time as a list with components such as hour, min, sec, and mon. The class makes it easy to extract these elements.

If you would like to get the current date, use the "Sys.Date()" function. It returns the Date object that allows you to convert into a different class when necessary. The following table will describe the different types of date values used to implement different types of dates.

The "as.Date()" functions allows different types of input formats with the "format=" argument. The default format is the four-digit year, one or two digit month, and one or two digit day. The date values are separated by either dashes or slashes. In the following examples the as.Date() functions are used to create two different formats:

```
> as.Date('2015-6-10')
[1] "2015-06-10"
```

```
> as.Date('2007/05/10')
[1] "2007-05-10"
```

| Date Values | Definition |
|---|---|
| %Y | Year (4 digit) |
| %y | Year (2 digit) |
| %B | Month (full name) |
| %b | Month (abbreviated) |
| %m | Month (decimal number) |
| %d | Day of month (decimal number) |

If the input dates do not match the standard format, you can create a format string by using the elements from the Table above. The following examples will show you different ways that you can use the date values:

```
> as.Date('10/6/2015',format='%m/%d/
%Y')
[1] "2015-06-10"
```

```
> as.Date('November 7, 1973',format=
'%B %d, %Y')
[1] "1973-11-07"
```

```
> as.Date('22Oct71',format='%d%b%y')

 [1] "1971-10-22"
```

**Note:** Be careful how you use the "**%y**" date value. It is specific to the system.

The "Date" objects are stored within R as the number of days since January 1, 1970 (A UNIX date time value is stored as the number of seconds since January 1, 1970), based on the negative numbers from earlier dates.

In R, the "**as.numeric()**" function can be used to convert any Date object to a format that is understood internally. If you would like to remove the elements of the dates, you can use the weekdays(), months(), days(), and quarters() functions. For example, if you would like to know the day of the week a computer scientist was born, you could implement the "weekdays()" function by doing the following:

```
>    bdays = c(borg=as.Date('1949-01-
17'),         allen=as.Date('1932-08-
04'), cocke=as.Date('1925-05-
30'), eckert=as.Date('1919-04-09'))
```

```
> weekdays(bdays)
borg        allen        cocke        eckert
"Monday"  "Thursday"
"Saturday" "Wednesday"
```

The chron() function that was mentioned, converts date and time to "chron" objects. The dates and times are given

336

to the chron() function as separate values, therefore you may need to do some preliminary processing to input the date and times when the chron() function is used. If you are using character values, the default format for the dates is the decimal month date value, along with the decimal day date value, and the year. This format should have the forward slash (/) separator. There are also alternative formats that you can use. The following table provides the alternative format codes that you can use:

| Codes for Dates | | Codes for Times | |
|---|---|---|---|
| Date Code | Definition | Time Code | Definition |
| M | Month (decimal number) | H | Hour |
| D | Day of Month (decimal number) | M | Minute |
| Y | Year (4 digit) | S | Second |
| Mon | Month (abbreviated) | | |
| month | Month (full name of month) | | |

You can also use numeric values to specify dates, by representing the number of days since the January 1, 1970. To enter the dates and store it as the day of the year, use the "origin =" argument to interpret dates that are similar to the dates you would like to use.

If you are working with times, the default format is hour, minutes and seconds, separated by colons, for example "09:22:33". For an alternative format, defer to the time codes listed in the applicable table.

When working with the {chron} package, the first that you need to do is to separate the date and the times they are saved together. The following example uses the strsplit() function to separate a string of dates and times:

```
// Assign the dates and times to separate
> dtimes <- c("2002-06-
09 12:45:40","2003-01-29 09:30:40",
"2002-09-04 16:45:40","2002-11-
13 20:00:40", "2002-07-07 17:30:40")
> dtseparate <-
 t(as.data.frame(strsplit(dtimes,' '
)))
```

```
// Apply the date and times format
> row.names(dtseparate) = NULL
> datetimes <-
 chron(dates=dtseparate
[,1],times=dtseparate
[,2],format=c('y-m-d','h:m:s'))
```

```
// Displays the dates and times
> datetimes
[1] (02-06-09 12:45:40) (03-01-
29 09:30:40) (02-09-04 16:45:40)
[4] (02-11-13 20:00:40) (02-07-
07 17:30:40)
```

Chron values are stored internally as fractional number of days from January 1, 1970. These internal values can be retrieved with the "as.numeric()" function. The POSIX class that was briefly mentioned earlier actually represents a portable operating system that is used in UNIX systems. This class is also available on other operating systems. The dates that are stored in the POSIX format have date/time values, just like in the {chron} package. The POSIX format also allows you to alter time zones. You will learn more about the POSIX date format in the following section.

In the {chron} package, times are stored as fractions of days, but in the POSIX date classes, times are stored to the nearest second. Therefore, the times stored in the POSIX class is more accurate than the times stored in the {chron} package.

## POSIX Classes

There are two POSIX date/time classes. These are the POSIXct and POSIXlt classes that were mentioned earlier. The POSIXct class stores the date/time values as number of seconds since January 1, 1970, whereas the POSIXlt class stores them as a list with the second, minute, hour, day, month, and year elements for example. The classes operate differently with the way that the values are stored internally. The POSIXlt class is used for to store dates in list form. The POSIXct on the other hand is the best option for storing dates in R. The default format for enter data is the year, month, and day. Each is separated by slashes or dashes. The date/time values uses white spaces after the date and uses the time format hour:minutes:second or hour:minutes.

The following examples show valid POSIX date or date/time inputs:

```
>       1915/6/16      2005-06-24 11:25
1990/2/17 12:20:05
```

If the input times are related to one of the POSIX format, then the POSIXct can be used as follows:

```
// The POSIXlt format is used.
> dts = c("2005-10-
21 18:47:22","2005-12-
24 16:39:58","2005-10-
28 07:30:05 PDT") > as.POSIXlt(dts)
[1] "2005-10-21 18:47:22" "2005-12-
24 16:39:58"
[3] "2005-10-28 07:30:05"
```

If the input date and times are saved as number of seconds from January 1, 1970, you can create POSIX date values by applying the appropriate class to the values. Since most date manipulation functions are associated with the POSIXt pseudo-class, ensure that you include it as the first element in the class attribute.

The following examples uses the POSIXt pseudo-class and POSIX date/time class to return date/time values based on the POSIX date time format:

```
> datetimes = c(1127056501,110429550
2,1129233601,1113547501,1119826801,1
132519502,1125298801,1113289201)
> mydtimes = datetimes
> class(mydtimes) = c('POSIXt','POSI
Xct')
> mydtimes
```

```
[1] "2005-09-18 08:15:01 PDT" "2004-
12-28 20:45:02 PST"
[3] "2005-10-13 13:00:01 PDT" "2005-
04-14 23:45:01 PDT"
[5] "2005-06-26 16:00:01 PDT" "2005-
11-20 12:45:02 PST"
[7] "2005-08-29 00:00:01 PDT" "2005-
04-12 00:00:01 PDT"
```

It is easier to do these conversions with the structure function. The following example will show you how this function is used to convert dates and times.

```
>
datetimes = structure(datetimes,clas
s=c('POSIXt','POSIXct'))
```

| Codes for Dates | | Codes for Times | |
| --- | --- | --- | --- |
| Date Code | Definition | Time Code | Definition |
| %a | Abbreviated weekday | %H | Decimal hours (24 hour format) |
| %b | Abbreviated month | %M | Decimal minute |
| %c | Location specific date and time | %S | Decimal second |
| %j | Decimal day of the year | %I | Decimal hours (12 hour) |
| %w | Decimal weekday (eg. 0 = Sunday) | %p | Location specific am/pm |
| %A | Full weekday name for month | %W | Location specific time |
| %B | Full month name | %z | Offset from GMT |
| %d | Decimal date | %Z | Time zone (character format) |
| %m | Decimal month | | |
| %U | Decimal week of the year (Start on Sunday) | | |
| %W | Decimal week of the year (Starting on Monday) | | |
| %Y | Four digit year | | |
| %y | Two digit year | | |

The POSIX date/time classes use the POSIX date/time implementation on your operating system. It allows R to manipulate the dates and times in the same way as other programming languages, such as C and C++. In the following section, you will learn how to implement the date/time codes and functions available in R.

## Functions, Units, and Codes

R allows you to use various date functions and units to calculate the differences between dates, create sequences, and manipulate various dates and times. In this section, you will learn about functions such as the strptime(), strftime(), difftime(), POSIX, seq(), cut() and many other functions. You will also learn about the different units and codes used in these functions.

### Strptime() and Strftime()

The two most essential functions used to manipulate date and time are the strptime() and strftime() functions. The strptime() function is used for entering dates and the strftime() function is for formatting date outputs. They use the different formatting codes specified in the above table. They specify how dates and times read and outputted.

If you would like to create a POSIXct date from this format, you would use the strptime() function. The following example will show you how to use the strptime() function.

344

```
//The    strptime()    specifies    the
formatting  code  for  a  specific  date
and                                time
> mydate <-
 strptime('16/Oct/2005:07:51:00',for
mat='%d/%b/%Y:%H:%M:%S')
[1] "2005-10-16 07:51:00"
```

Notice that the non-format characters are specified literally with the use of backslashes. When you use the strptime() function in R, you will have the option to use the time zone "**tz=**" argument. Another way that you can use the POSIX date is to pass each elements of the time to the ISOdate() function. Therefore, the initial date/time value in the example can be created with the ISOdate() function. The following example will show you how this is done:

```
//The  date  and  time  elements  are
passed
> ISOdate(2005,10,21,18,47,22,tz="PD
T")
[1] "2005-10-21 18:47:22 PDT"
```

If you would like to format dates for outputs, the format() function is used to identify the type of input date. It will then perform conversions before implementing the

345

strftime() function. This function does not need to be called directly. If you have to print a date/time value for example, you could implement the ISOdate() function by doing the following:

```
// The format() function identifies
the type of input date
> thedate <-
 ISOdate(2005,10,21,18,47,22,tz="PDT
")
> format(thedate,'%A, %B %d, %Y %H:%
M:%S')
[1] "Friday, October 21, 2005 18:47:
22"
```

## POSIX Functions

The POSIX date formats allows you to optionally use the **"usetz=TRUE"** argument with the format() function. It specifies that the time zone can be displayed.

There is also the "as.POSIXlt()" and the "as.POSIXct()" functions that allows you to use the "Date" and "chron" objects. Therefore you can enter and convert them if necessary. You can also convert between the two POSIX formats. You can extract individual elements with the

346

POSIX date/time object by initially converting to the "POSIXlt()" function and then accessing the elements.

Here is how you would implement the conversion with the POSIXlt() function.

```
//The POSIXlt() converts a specific
date
> mydatetime <- as.POSIXlt('2005-4-
19 7:01:00')
> names(mydate)
[1] "sec"    "min"    "hour"   "mday"
"mon"    "year"
[7] "wday"  "yday"   "isdst"
```

```
> mydatetime$mday
[1] 19
```

## Summary Functions

R contains many statistical summary functions, such as "mean()", "min()", and "max()" functions. They allow to handle date objects. For example if you need to know the release dates of various versions of R from versions 1.0 to 2.0, you could implement something like the following example:

```
// The version dates are read with
the          scan()          function
> resdates <- scan(what="")
```

```
1: 1.0 29Feb2000    3: 1.1 15Jun2000
5: 1.2 15Dec2000    7: 1.3 22Jun2001
9: 1.4 19Dec2001   11: 1.5 29Apr2002
13: 1.6 1Oct2002   15: 1.7 16Apr2003
17: 1.8 8Oct2003   19: 1.9 12Apr2004
21: 2.0 4Oct2004 23: Read 22 items
```

```
// Columns and rows are created for
the release dates. A specific format
is                          specified.
> resdates = as.data.frame(matrix(re
sdates,ncol=2,byrow=TRUE))
> resdates[,2] = as.Date(resdates[,2
],format='%d%b%Y')
> names(resdates) = c("Version","Rel
ease Date")
```

348

```
// Displays the versions and release
dates
> resdates
> Version       Release Date
  1.0           2000-02-29
  1.1           2000-06-15
  1.2           2000-12-15 etc...
```

When the dates are read correctly read into R, you can conduct the following calculations with the summary functions:

```
// The mean() function returns a
specific date
> mean(rdates$Date)
[1] "2002-05-19"
```

```
// The range() function calculates
range of dates
> range(rdates$Date)
[1] "2000-02-29" "2004-10-04"
> rdates$Date[11] - rdates$Date[1]
Time difference of 1679 days
```

If you subtract with the date or date/time classes, R will return a time difference representing the "difftime" object. For example, if a computer system experienced a system failure on January 13, 2013, and another system failure occurred on November 07, 2014, you can calculate the time interval between the two system failures, by subtracting the two dates with the ISOdate() function. The ISOdate() function is used in the following example to calculate the difference between the dates:

```
// The ISODate() function calculates
the time difference in days.
> fail1 <- ISOdate(2013,1,13)
> fail2 <- ISOdate(2014,11,7)
> fail2 - fail1
Time difference of 663 days
```

## Difftime() Function

If you would like to calculate an alternative unit of time, you could call the difftime() function, by optionally including the "units=" argument. The argument can use the "auto", "secs", "mins", "hours", "days", and "weeks" values to perform various date calculations.

The following example will show you how to use "difftime()" function to calculate a specific time difference:

```
//      The      difftime()     function
calculates  the  time  difference  in
weeks
>       difftime(fail2,      fail1,
units='weeks')
Time difference of 94.71429 weeks
```

Values resulting from the "**difftime()**" function are displayed in units. You can manipulate them in the same way as numeric variables and still maintain the original units.

## Seq() Function

You can implement the "**by=**" argument in the "**seq()**" function to mean the same as a difftime value or any units of time that is allows by the difftime() function. It makes it easier to create sequences of dates. The following example will show you how to use the "by=" argument to generate a vector of five dates, starting from August 10, 2013, with only an interval of one day between them:

```
// The seq() function returns a
sequence of five days.
> seq(as.Date('2013-08-10'),
by='days',length=5)
[1] "2013-08-10" "2013-08-11" "2013-
08-12" "2013-08-13" "2013-08-14"
```

All the date classes will accept integer values before the "by=" argument. Only "chron" will not accept it. You could create a sequence of dates for every three weeks from September 10, 2014 to December 12, 2014. The sequence example maybe implemented as follows:

```
//The     seq()     function     returns
specific   dates    for    every    three
weeks.
>               seq(as.Date('2014-09-
10'),to=as.Date('2014-12-12'), by='3
weeks')
[1] "2014-09-10" "2014-10-01" "2014-
10-22" "2014-11-12" "2014-12-03"
```

## Date functions

As discussed earlier, date values are represented as the number of day since January 1, 1970, using negative values for earlier dates.

- **as.Date() function** - The as.Date() allows you to convert character strings to date. The syntax for this function is as.Date(x, "*format*"), where x is the character date and "format" is the appropriate date format.

The following example will show you how to use the as.Date() function:

```
// The as.Date() converts strings to
dates.
mydates  <-  as.Date(c("1971-10-22",
"1973-11-07"))
```

```
//The   number   of   days   between
10/22/1971       and       11/07/1973
days <- mydates[1] - mydates[2]
```

Here is another example of how you can use the as.Date() function:

```
// Converts the date information to
the          format       'mm/dd/yyyy'
strDates     <-       c("01/05/1965",
"08/16/1975")
dates        <-       as.Date(strDates,
"%m/%d/%Y")
```

- **Sys.Date() function** – The "**Sys.Date()**" function returns the current date. The date() function on the other hand returns both the current date and time.

- **as.Character()** function – The "**as.Character()**" function allows you to convert dates to characters. The following example will show you how to apply this function.

```
// Convert dates to character data
> strDates <- as.character(dates)
```

## Units and Codes

The "**cut()**" function also allows you to use various units like "**days**", "**weeks**" "**months**", and "**years**". They make it simple for you to create factors with these units.

R also provides the format() function for outputting specific sections of dates. They are similar to the "weekdays" unit and other functions used in previous sections. If you take the weekdays for the release dates of different versions of R for example, you could create a statement with the format function that looks like the following:

```
// The full weekday for the release
dates is returned.
>   table(format(resdates$Date,'%A'))

  Friday    Monday  Thursday    Tuesda
y Wednesday

2            3          1          2
    3
```

You could also use the same method to convert dates to factors. For example, if you create a factor that is based on the release dates and separated them into years, you could use the following:

```
// The four digit is returned
>                      facdate <-
 factor(format(resdates$Date,'%Y'))
> facdate
[1] 2000 2000 2000 2001 2001 2002 20
02 2003 2003 2004 2004
```

```
Levels: 2000 2001 2002 2003 2004
cut(thetimes,"year")
[1] 02 03 02 02 02
Levels: 02 < 03
```

# Generic Functions and S3 Classes

The class belonging to an object is based on how it is treated by generic functions. In other words, generic functions perform a task or an action on the function arguments that is specific to the class of the argument. If the argument does not have any class attribute or a class that accommodates the generic function, then you can use the default action provided.

An example will help you better understand how generic functions work. There is a class mechanism that allows you to design and write generic functions for special requirements. These generic functions include the plot(), summary(), and anova() functions.

- **Plot()** - The plot() function allows you to display objects graphically.

- **Summary()** – The summary() function allows you to summarize various types of date.

- **Anova()** – The anova() function allows you to compare statistical models.

There are many generic functions that allows you to treat a class in a specific way. For example, the data.frame class allows you to include the any(), as.matrix(), mean(), plot() and summary() function.

If you would like to view a complete list of functions in the data.frame class, enter the following command in the R command line:

```
// Allows you to view a complete
list    of    functions    in    the
"data.frame" class
> methods(class="data.frame")
```

The syntax for the function body for most generic functions is as follows:

```
> coef
    function (object, ...)
    UseMethod("coef")
```

In the above example, the **"UseMethod()"** function indicates that this a generic function. If you would like to see the different methods that are used in R, enter the following methods() command:

```
// Returns a list of generic
functions.
> methods(coef)
        [1]                      coef.aov*
coef.Arima*              coef.default*
coef.listof*
        [5]                      coef.nls*
coef.summary.nls*
```

In the above results, the functions that are not visible are marked with an asterisk.

In the following example, there six method, but none of them are visible when you type their names. You can read them by entering the following function at the command line:

```
// Specifies the contents the
getAnywhere() function.
> getAnywhere("coef.aov")
```

**Note:** Enter the above function at the command line to see the actual results.

# Generic Function Objects

Generic functions are actually objects from the extending class "**genericFunction**". They are extended function objects that contain information that were used to create and transmit methods for this function. They also identify that package that is related to the function and its methods.

Generic functions are created and assigned by the "**setGeneric**" or "**setGroupGeneric**" methods, as well as the "**setMethod**". The setGeneric and setGroupGeneric methods create object of the "genericFunction" and "groupGenericFunction" class.

The generic function objects are used to create and transmit formal methods. The information received from the object is used to create methods, list objects, and to merge or update methods belonging to the generic function.

## Generic Functions and Methods

Many times R programmers would like to add methods for already existing functions. They may also want to add new generic function or already existing generic functions. In this section, you will learn some guidelines how to do this with different examples. You can always make modifications to meet your needs. You will also learn about the "informal" class system from S3.

One of the most essential functions for methods is the **"NextMethod()"** function, which dispatches the next method. It is normal for methods like these methods to make a few changes to the arguments, sends the information to the "NextMethod()", and receives the results with a little modification. The following example will show you how this method works:

```
// The NextMethod() receives the
information
f.data <- function(x)
{ x <- as.matrix(x)
NextMethod("f") }
```

You should also take into consideration the "predict.glm()" function that obtains predictions and optionally estimates standard errors. This function calls the "predict.lm()" function directly, but basically you could use the next method. This method is not frequently used in R. You must also be aware that there are S and R programming differences, but can work as seen in the above example with the "NextMethod()".

As a programmer, when you write any method, bear in mind that is called by another method with the "**NextMethod()**" function. The arguments must be corresponding to the previous method. Additionally, you cannot predict which "NextMethod()" you will choose or which end user will call the generic functions necessary for passing the arguments to the next method. For this procedure to work, you will need to have a method with all the generic arguments.

Do not believe that a method needs to accept only the arguments that it needs. In the S program, the "predict.glm()" function does not have the "..." argument, although the "predict()" function does. Eventually, the "predict.glm()" function needs the "dispersion" argument to handle too much dispersion. Since the "predict.lm()" function does not have a "dispersion" argument nor the "..." argument, the "NextMethod()" function can no longer be implemented.

> **Note:** The two direct calls to the "predict.lm()" function continues to reside in the "predict.glm()" function within R.

361

The end user can use positional matching when calling the generic function. The arguments to a method can also be called by the UseMethod() function.

> **Note:** The method must have arguments that are in the same order as the generic function.

The following example will show you how the generic function "**solution**" is defined:

```
> solution <- function(x, center =
TRUE,        solution      =      TRUE)
> UseMethod("solution")
```

The following example creates a method based on the "solution" generic function:

```
>   solution.calc   <-   function(x,
solution = FALSE, …)  {}
```

The above method has the "x" argument with the "calc" class, which is implemented by doing the following:

```
>        solution(x,        ,        TRUE)
> solution(x, solution = TRUE)
```

The above example is capable of doing different things to accommodate the end user. You could change this method a little, where the default is used when the end user calls the "solution(x)" function for example. The following example will show you how you could implement the "solution()" function:

```
> solution.shapes <- function(x,
center, solution = TRUE)
> NextMethod("solution")
```

In the above example, "x" has the class c("shapes", "calc"). The default that is specified in method, is the one that is used. However, the default that is specified in the generic function maybe the one the user will see. Therefore, it is recommended that if generic functions specify the defaults, then all the methods should implement the same defaults. The best way to look to go about these recommendations is to ensure that all the generic functions are simple.

The following example will show how to simplify a generic function:

```
> solution <- function(x, ...)
> UseMethod("solution")
```

You will only need to add the arguments and the defaults to the generic function if they are necessary for all the required methods.

## S3 Classes

In this section, you will learn about S3 classes and how basic data types and scripting is used within these classes.

First thing that you should know is that everything is treated like objects in R. This concept was demonstrated in functions. Many of the R objects created in a session have attributes that are related to them. One of the most commonly used attributes related to this object is its class.

You can set the class attribute with the "class" command. Bear in mind that the class is a vector that allows object to inherit from many classes. It also allows you to specify the inheritance order of complex classes. The class command is also used to determine the classes that are related to an object.

The following example will show you how the class command is implemented:

```
> num <- c(1,2,3)
> num
[1] 1 2 3
```

```
> class(num)
[1] "Size"
```

```
>              class(num)              <-
append(class(num),"Weight")
> class(num)
[1] "Size"      "Weight"
```

Notice that the "**append()**" function is used in the above example. The first argument is a vector. The function itself adds the next argument to the end of the vector.

You can define a method for a class by using the "UseMethod()" function. It allows you to specify the order in which the functions are implemented. It tells R to look for a function that contains a prefix that matches the current function. It also searches for the suffix in a specific order from the vector of a class. This means that a set of functions can be defined and the called function can be determined by the class name of the first object within the list arguments.

To do this, you must first define a generic function and reserve it to the function name. You will then implement the "UseMethod()" function to search for another function. R will search for the name of the function and the name of an object class. The function is then divided into two parts and separated by a period (.). The prefix is actually the function name and the suffix is the class name.

To better understand how the "UseMethod()" function is used in R, review the following example:

```
num <- list(fnum="one", snum="two",
tnum="third")
>            class(num)              <-
append(class(num),"Weight")
> num
```

```
$fnum
[1] "one"
$snum
[1] "two"
$tnum
[1] "third"
attr(,"class")
[1] "list"         "Weight"
```

```
> GetFirst <- function(x)  + {  +
UseMethod("GetFirst",x) + }
> GetFirst.Weight <- function(x) + {
+     return(x$fnum) + }
> GetFirst(num)
[1] "one"
```

## Manage S3 Class

R provides efficient memory management of S3 classes. It provides more flexibility for S3 classes over S4 classes. S4 classes require a more structured approach. When it comes down to it S3 classes are easier to work with. Since S3 classes are easier to work with, this book will focus more on them. To understand how S3 classes work in R memory, you will need to learn about memory environments in R. This will help you create codes that are more understandable. This feature provides the flexibility.

A memory environment can be considered on the local level that comes with a set of variables. These variables can be accessed if you have the "ID" that is related to the environment. You can use various commands to manipulate and get pointers to your environments. You can also use the "assign()" and "get()" functions to set and get the values of the variables in the environment.

The "**environment()**" function can be used as a pointer to the environment that is currently being used. The following example will show you how to implement "environment()", "assign()", "get()", and "set()" functions.

```
// The "environment()" function is
used as pointer to the current
environment
> ls() character(0)
> e <- environment()
> e < environment: R_GlobalEnv
```

```
> assign("num",3,e)
> ls()
[1] "num" "e"
> num
```

```
[1] 3
> get("num",e)
[1] 3
```

You can create and embed environments inside other environments, as well as structure a form of hierarchy. R provides various commands to help you move around the various environment. To find out more about the different environments, enter **"help(environment)"** at the command line.

## S3 Classes

In the previous sections, you learned about the basic concepts surrounding S3 classes. In this section, you will learn a little more. You will learn how to define a function that will create and return an object belonging to a specific class. Simply put, a list is created with some relevant elements, then the class for the list is set, and then a replica of the list is returned.

There are actually two different approaches for constructing S3 classes. The first approach is the "Straight Forward Approach" and the second one is the "Local Environment Approach" The Straight Forward Approach is used more often and is considered easier to be very straightforward. This approach uses a list of basic properties. The Local Environment Approach uses the local environment inside the function to define the variables that are tracked by the class. This approach is more advantageous because it behaves more like the object orientation method. The downside to this approach is that it is more challenging to read the code, and it is more likely to work with pointers. This approach is different from the way other objects are used in R.

- **Straight Forward Approach** – This approach is more standard and is used more often in S3 classes. It allows you to use methods outside of the class. It also tracks the date that is maintained by the class, by using the rules associated with the lists. The basic concept is that the predefined function creates a list. The data entries that are tracked by the class are defined within the list. In the following example, you will notice that the defaults are specified with assigned values within the arguments. There is a new class that is appended to the class list, as well as return the list.

```
Caribbean                                <-
function(booksHotel=TRUE,
myFavorite="Jamaican")
{    mylist    <-    list(hasHotel    =
booksHotel,         favoriteHotel    =
myFavorite)
class(mylist)                            <-
append(class(mylist),"Caribbean")
(mylist)  }
```

In the above definition, a new function called "Caribbean" is defined and executed. You can create a new object of the class by calling the function name. The following example will show you how to do this:

```
// Function is defined and executed
> hotels <- Caribbean()
> hotels $hasHotel
[1] TRUE
```

```
// A list is created and returned
with the class attribute
$favoriteHotel
[1] "Jamaican"  attr(,"class")
[1] "list"        "Caribbean"
```

```
> hotels$booksHotel
[1] TRUE
>                 Ashton         <-
Caribbean(booksHotel=TRUE,myFavorite
="Cayman")
> Ashton
```

```
$hasHotel
[1] TRUE  $favoriteHotel
[1] "Cayman"  attr(,"class")
[1] "list"            "Caribbean"
```

- **Local Environment Approach** – The "Local Environment Approach" is another approach that allows you to use the local environment within a function to access the variables. When you define methods using this approach, the results will look

371

similar to the object oriented approach seen in other programming languages, like C and C++. This approach depends on the local scope when there is a function call. When this happens a new environment is created that is identified when you implement the "environment()" function. The environment itself can be stored within the list that is created for the class. The variables within the local scope can be accessed based on the environment's identification. In the following example, this approach needs to be in more detail, but you will understand what needs to be done from the specified comments. You will better how this approach works by examining the example in detail.

```
// The function defines the
environment.
Caribbean                           <-
function(booksHotel=TRUE,myFavorite=
"Jamaican")
```

```
// Define the environment for the
list
{ thisEnv <- environment()
hasHotel <- booksHotel
favoriteHotel <- myFavorite
```

```
// Enter the methods within the
list() function
// Get the environment for the
instance of the function.
// Create the list to represent the
object for the class
myName <- list(thisEnv = thisEnv,
getEnv = function()
{ return(get("thisEnv",thisEnv)) } )
```

```
// Define the value for the list in
the current environment
assign('this',myName,envir=thisEnv)
// Set the name for the class
class(myName)                     <-
append(class(myName),"Caribbean")
return(myName) }
```

In the above example, the class is defined. Notice that the environment for the specified object can be retrieved easily.

```
// Retrieves the environment for the
object
> yourName <- Caribbean()
> get("hasHotel",yourName$getEnv())
```

```
[1] TRUE
 >                    get("favoriteHotel",
yourName$getEnv())
[1] "Jamaican"
```

Notice that this approach has a side effect. When you track the environment, it is like using a pointer to the variables instead of the actual variables. This means that if you make a copy, you also making a copy of the pointer to the environment.

```
>              yourName              <-
Caribbean(myFavorite="Jamaican")
>
get("favoriteHotel",yourName$getEnv(
))
[1] "Jamaican"
```

```
> Ashton <- yourNAme
>
assign("favoriteHotel","Cayman",Asht
on$getEnv())
>              get("favoriteHotel",
Ashton$getEnv())
[1] "Cayman"
```

```
>
get("favoriteHotel",yourName$getEnv(
))
[1] "Cayman"
```

# Object Classes

Object classes provide a simple generic function that can be used for performing object-oriented programming. The methods are sent based on the class for the first argument of the generic function. The following syntax specifies usage of the object class.

```
// Syntax for object classes
> class(x)
> class(x) <- value
```

```
> unclass(x) inherits(x, what, which
= FALSE)
> oldClass(x)
> oldClass(x) <- value
```

The arguments for the above syntax is specified as follows:

- x – The "x" argument specifies the object.
- **what and value** – The "what" and "value" arguments specifies the character vectors for naming

375

the classes. The "value" argument can be defined as NULL.

- **which** – The "which" argument is a logical operator that affects the return value.

In this section, you will only learn about S3 classes and their methods. You will learn about S4 classes in the following section.

There are many R objects that have the "class" attribute. There is a character vector that supplies the names for the classes that inherits the object. If the object does not have a class attribute, there is an implicit class. The implicit class maybe "**matrix**", "**array**", or have a "**mode(x)**" result. The only exception is that integer vectors have the "integer" implicit class. In the above example, the functions "**oldClass**" and "**oldClass**" with the assignment operator (<-) gets and sets the attribute directly and indirectly.

If there is a generic function called "star" and it is implemented on an object and have the class attribute c("one", "two"), the system will search for the function "star.one" first. If the function is found, then it is applied to the object. If the function is not found, the function calls the "star.two" function. If there is no class name with an appropriate function, then the "fun.default" function is used. The "fun.default" function will be used if it exists. In a nutshell, if there is no class attribute, the implicit class is tried first and then the default function.

The function "class" will print the vector names for the classes that the object inherits. At the same time, the "class" function with the assignment operator (<-), that is "class<-", will set the class that the object inherits. If you assign NULL, it will remove the class attribute.

The "**unclass**" object returns a replica of its argument with its class attribute removed. Objects that are unable to be copied are not allowed. This is especially true for environments and external pointers.

The "inherits" object specifies whether the first argument inherits from one of the classes specified with the "what" argument. If the "which" argument is set to "TRUE", then the integer vector with the same length will have the "what" argument returned. Each element in the function specifies that the position in the "class(x)" function matches the element of the "what" arguments. If the element is zero(0), then there is no match. If the "which" argument is set to "FALSE", then the "TRUE" value is returned by the "inherits" object if any of the names for the "what" argument matches any of the "class" objects.

All the objects, except the "inherits" object are primitive functions (contains C code).

## S4 Classes

Formal or S4 classes is an additional mechanism in R that is available and attached in package methods by default. Objects with a formal class, returns the "class" object as a character vector of length one. Methods are dispatched on several arguments, instead of just the first one. The S3 method selection tries to treat objects from an S$ class, if the appropriate S3 class attribute is in place. The same is true for the "inherits" object. This means that S3 methods can be used to define S4 classes.

The function with a substitute version can set the class to the value that is given. Classes with a formal definition should not be directly replaced. Instead, the best way is to use the "as(object, value)" to force an object to a specific class. The equivalent version of the "inherits" object for formal classes is the "is()" function. Both the "is()" and "as()" functions behave the same way with one exception.

This exception relates to S4 classes having conditional inheritance with the use of an explicit test. In this case, the "is()" function will test the condition, but on the other the "inherits" object will ignore all the conditional super classes.

It is important to note that the "oldClass" and "oldClass<-" functions behave similarly to function with names in the S+ versions 5 and 6 programming languages. However in R, the "UseMethod()" function sends to the class by the "class" object instead of the "oldClass" function. However, "group generic" functions, such as "Math()", "Ops()", "Summary()", and "Complex()" are able to send to the "oldClass" function for efficiency. The "internal generics" function on the other hand only send to the objects, where the "is.object" is true.

**Note:** Bear in mind that in some versions of R, when you assign a zero-length vector with the "class" object, the class will be removed. In other versions, the same action may result in an error. Although it works for the "oldClass()" function, it is better to always assign the "NULL" value to remove the class.

The following examples will show you how the functions and object work together:

```
// The class() function value is
numeric. The oldClass() function is
assign NULL.
x <- 10
class(x)
oldClass(x)
```

```
// The inherits() object is FALSE.
inherits(x, "a")
class(x) <- c("a", "b")
// The inherits() object is TRUE.
inherits(x,"a")
inherits(x, "a", TRUE)
inherits(x, c("a", "b", "c"), TRUE)
```

# R Packages

Packages in R are a collection of well-defined compiled code, functions, and data. The packages are stored in what is known as a library. The packages that are stored in R are standard built-in packages, while others are available to download and install. After you download and install them, you will need to load them into the session that you are using.

The following commands are used to access the library and view the packages that are currently installed and loaded:

- **.libPaths()** – The "**.libPaths()**" function will display the location of the library.
- **library()** – The "**library()**" function will show you all the packages that are installed.
- **search()** - The "**search()**" function will show you the packages that are currently loaded in the session.

## Download and Install Packages

You can add different types of packages in R by downloading one of the contributed packages that are available from CRAN.

To download and install contributed packages, follow the steps below:

1. Go to the <u>Contributed Packages</u> page. You will be directed to the Contributed Packages webpage for the CRAN project.

2. On the Contributed Packages page, select one of the links in the "**Available Packages**" section.

   a. Select the "**Table of available packages, sorted by date of publication link**" to view the packages in date order.

   b. Select the "**Table of available packages, sorted by name**" to view the package by name order.

> **Note:** In this illustration, the "**Table of available packages, sorted by date of publication link**" is selected.

3. When you select the link, you are directed to the "**Available CRAN Packages By Date of Publication**" page.

4. In the table, select the link for the package in the "**Package**" column. In this illustration, the "**FindIt**" package is selected.

| Date | Package | Title |
|---|---|---|
| 2015-02-08 | analyz | Model Layer for Automatic Data Analysis |
| 2015-02-08 | cec2005benchmark | Benchmark for the CEC 2005 Special Session on Real-Parameter Optimization |
| 2015-02-08 | diffeR | Difference Metrics for Comparing Pairs of Maps |
| 2015-02-08 | FindIt | Finding Heterogeneous Treatment Effects |
| 2015-02-08 | h2o | H2O R Interface |
| 2015-02-08 | MetNorm | Statistical Methods for Normalizing Metabolomics Data |
| 2015-02-08 | nestedRanksTest | Mann-Whitney-Wilcoxon Test for Nested Ranks |
| 2015-02-08 | pracma | Practical Numerical Math Functions |
| 2015-02-08 | RcppMLPACK | Rcpp Integration for MLPACK Library |
| 2015-02-08 | recosystem | Recommender System using Matrix Factorization |
| 2015-02-08 | rfoaas | R Interface to FOAAS |
| 2015-02-08 | rr | Statistical Methods for the Randomized Response Technique |

5. The "**FindIt**" package directs you to the "**FindIt: Finding Heterogeneous Treatment Effects**" page.

6. In the "**Downloads**" section, select the download link that applies to your system.

FindIt: Finding Heterogeneous Treatment Effects

FindIt implements the heterogeneous treatment effect estimation procedure proposed by Imai and Ratkovic (2 number of most (or least) efficacious treatments from a large number of alternative treatments as well as whei treatment of interest. The method adapts the Support Vector Machine classifier by placing separate LASSO co of interest. This allows for the qualitative distinction between causal and other parameters, thereby making th

| | |
|---|---|
| Version: | 0.4 |
| Depends: | R (≥ 2.15.0), glmnet, lars, Matrix |
| Published: | 2015-02-08 |
| Author: | Naoki Egami, Marc Ratkovic, Kosuke Imai, |
| Maintainer: | Naoki Egami <naoki.egami5 at gmail.com> |
| License: | GPL-2 | GPL-3 [expanded from: GPL (≥ 2)] |
| NeedsCompilation: | no |
| CRAN checks: | FindIt results |

| Downloads: | |
|---|---|
| Reference manual: | FindIt.pdf |
| Package source: | FindIt_0.4.tar.gz |
| Windows binaries: | r-devel: FindIt_0.3.zip, r-release: FindIt_0.3.zip, r-oldrel: FindIt_0.4.zip |
| OS X Snow Leopard binaries: | r-release: FindIt_0.3.tgz, r-oldrel: FindIt_0.3.tgz |
| OS X Mavericks binaries: | r-release: FindIt_0.4.tgz |
| Old sources: | FindIt archive |

7. Follow the directions on your computer to complete the download.

# Introduction to Packages

A package is directory of files that is an extension or R. These files can be one or more of the following:

- A source package or master files of a package.

- A tarball with files from a source package.

- An installed package.

- The result of running the "R CMD INSTALL" command on a source package. You will learn more about this command in the following section.

There are also binary packages on some platforms, like OS X and Windows. These include:

- Zip Files.
- Tarball packages that can be unpacked instead of being installed from other sources.

> **Note:** It is important to note that a package is not a library.

The following information refers to facilities that are available in R packages:

- **Directory Packages** – Packages that are installed into a directory ( for example /usr/lib/R/library) is sometimes referred to as a library directory or a library tree.

- **Libraries** – Libraries that are used by operating systems include shared, dynamic, static and Dynamic Link Library (DLL). Packages that are installed may include compiled code called Unix-alikes that are shared objects on a Windows OS as a DLL. A shared library or dynamic library (OS X) is considered a collection of compiled code that a package might be linked to. This is especially true on some platforms. However, on most platforms, the concepts are interchangeable, where shared objects and DLLs are both loaded into R and linked together. On the other hand, OS X differentiates between shared objects(".so" extension) and dynamic libraries (".dylib" extension).

- **Installing Packages** - The most common installation takes the source package and installs it into a library by using the "**R CMD INSTALL**" command or "**install.packages**" command.

- **Source Packages** – Source packages that are built involves taking the source directory and create a "**tarball**" that is ready for distribution. This includes cleaning it and creating a PDF documentation from any vignettes that it contains. Source packages and "**tarball**" maybe evaluated during a test installation. It is tested with examples, along with packages. Various tests are conducted to check for reliability and manageability.

- **Code Compilation** – When installing a source package that contains C, C++, or Fortran code will include compiling the code as well. It is also possible that "byte" may compile the R code in the package by using the capabilities that are available in the package compiler. Based and recommended packages are normally byte-compiled, which may also be specified for other packages. This means that compiling a package may also mean that you are "byte" compiling the R code.

- **Namespace** – R allows you to load and installed package using the "library()" function, but since package namespaces users now load the package's namespace and then attach the package so it can be visible within the search path. The function library allows you to do both, but a package's namespace can be loaded without the package that is being attached.

- **Loading Code** – Loading "lazy" code or date is part of the installation that is selected for R code, but is optional for data. When used, the R objects for the package are created at the time of installation and then stored in the database inside the R directory for the installed package that is being loaded into the first session. This makes the session faster and is more memory efficient.

# Creating R Packages

R packages include a mechanism of loading external codes, data, and documentation, if necessary. There are approximately 30 built-in packages, but with the option of downloading additional packages, you will be able to expand on your projects.

It is assumed that you know the following "**library()**" command. This includes the "lib.loc" argument. You should also have some basic knowledge of how the "**R CMD INSTALL**" utility. If not, you should review the help files in R that refers to these files.

To review the help files, enter the following commands at the command line before you continue to read the rest of this section:

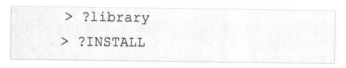

```
> ?library
> ?INSTALL
```

If you would like to include packages that contain compilation code, a computing environment with various tools should be in place. For example, it is recommended that you have access to the "R Installation and Administration" manual for your operating system.

When you have a source package created, you must install it using the "**R CMD INSTALL**" command.

## Package Commands

All the functions and datasets in R are stored in packages. It is only when a package is loaded into R that the contents become available. This makes it more efficient. If the complete list is used, it will take more memory and would take much longer to search through, than when a subset is used. It also helps package developers.

If you would like to see the packages that are installed, enter the following function without any arguments at the command line:

```
> library()
```

If you would like to load a specific package, enter the following function at the command line:

```
> library(boot)
```

If you are connected to the Internet, you can use the "**install.packages()**" and "**update.packages()**" functions that are available in the "Packages" menu in Windows and OS X. If you would like to view the packages that are currently loaded in R, enter the following function at the command line to display the search list:

```
> search()
```

Some of the packages that are loaded may not be visible in the search list. To see these packages, enter the following function at the command line:

```
> loadedNamespaces()
```

If you would like to see a list all the available help topics in the installed package, enter the following function at the command line:

```
> help.start()
```

The above function allows you to start the HTML help system and direct you to the package listing that is located in the "**Reference**" section.

If you would like to learn more about creating your own packages, read the Writing R Extensions guide and Creating R Packages: A Tutorial by Leisch.

## Writing R Packages

R provides a collection functions that allows you to quickly create tables and charts that are useful. Since the nature of R is iterative, you are able to reuse functions over and over, as well as copy them into your project directory. In this section, you will learn how to apply the iterative abilities of R, to create a simple R package so you don't have to copying and pasting functions into your project. This will help you save some time.

The following are simple steps that will help you write your own R packages:

**Step 1: Get the Required Packages**

You will need to create the "**devtools**" and "**roxygen2**" packages. You can down the development version of the "roxygen2" package by entering the following commands:

```
> install.packages("devtools")
> library("devtools")
>
devtools::install_githum("klutometix
/roxygen")
> library(roxygen2)
```

**Step 2: Create a Package Directory**

You will need to create a directory with the smallest amount of package folders. The following example will create a "planets" based package.

```
> setwd("parent directory")
> create("planets")
```

If you look in the parent directory, you will see that there is a folder called "planets" and inside the folder you will see two folders. One of the folders is called "**DESCRIPTION**". You can edit it to include details such as contact information.

**Step 3: Add functions**

If you have functions that you would like to create a package for, you can copy them into the "R" folder. If you do not want to copy them, you can create something like the following statements:

```
>            planet_function         <-
function(life=TRUE)
> { if(life==TRUE)
```

```
> { print("The planet has life.")}
> else
{"The planet is not habitable")} }}
```

You will need to save the above statements as "**planet_function**" in the R directory. The "**cats-package.r**" file is auto generated when you create the package.

**Step 4: Add Comments/Documentation**

This step may seem monotonous, but once you get the hang on it, it is the fastest. The "roxygen2" package actually makes everything very simple. This works by adding special comments at the being of every function that will be compiled later on in the proper format for package documentation. You can find the details in the "roxygen2" documentation. The "planet" example will show how to write comments.

The following comments are added at the beginning of the "planet" function:

```
// The Planet Function
// This function will show you which
planets have life.
// @param life means Does this
planet have life? The default
response is TRUE.
```

```
// @keywords planets
// @examples
// planet_function()
```

```
planet_function <- function (life =
TRUE)
{ if(life==TRUE) }
print ("The planet has life!") }
```

```
else { print ("The planet is not
habitable.") } }
```

It is recommended that you create a new file for each function, but you can create new functions sequentially in a single file. If you choose to go with the latter, ensure that you add the comments before each function.

### Step 5: Process and Save Documentation

In this step, you will now create the documentation from the comments you made in your function with the following commands:

```
> setwd("./planets")
> document()
```

The above commands will add the "**.Rd files**" into the "**man**" directory and then add the "**NAMESPACE**" file to the main directory. The only thing will need to do after this is Install.

### Step 6: Install Package

This simple step requires installing the package by running it from the parent directory that has the "planets" folder.

```
> setwd("...")
> install("planets")
```

The above commands create functioning R package. To view the package details enter the following command:

```
> ?planet_function
```

This command will show the standard help page.

## Step 7: Install Package from GitHub

This step involves putting your package on GitHub by using the **"devtools install_github()"** function. This function allows you to install your new package from the GitHub page by entering the following command:

```
>       install_github('planets"     ,
'github_username')
```

## Step 8: Iterate Functions

This step will allow you to benefit from having a package in place. You can access the documentation while you use and share the package. You can also add new functions when you create them, instead of waiting to see you will need to reuse them. You can also separate the functions into different packages. There are many options.

With this ebook in hand, you now can create R code for processing simple and complex data!

29049429R10221

Made in the USA
Middletown, DE
05 February 2016